Two Ozark Rivers

Two Ozark Rivers
The Current and the Jacks Fork

Photographs by Oliver Schuchard

Text by Steve Kohler

University of Missouri Press

Columbia, 1984

For Peg—Who Saw the Tree Fall

and for Matthew

Library of Congress Cataloging in Publication Data

Schuchard, Oliver.
    Two Ozark rivers, the Current and the Jacks Fork.

    Bibliography: p. 125
    1. Current River (Mo. and Ark.)—Description and
travel.   2. Jacks Fork (Mo.)—Description and travel.
I. Kohler, Steve.   II. Title.
F472.C9S38   1984   917.67'1   83-23554
ISBN 0–8262–0421–X

Preface

Among the hopes for any book conceived in the style of *Two Ozark Rivers* must be, first, that it does justice to its subject matter. It must aim to set out clearly and honestly the important details that make up the whole. Any art involved in such an endeavor comes not in embellishing or elaborating on the natural but in finding ways to set down on paper the qualities that make the places what they are, the singularities that make them special. In this instance, the subject is 130 miles of the Current and the Jacks Fork rivers, along with the surrounding watershed, situated deep in the Missouri Ozarks.

With that goal established for the book, the rivers become demanding taskmasters. To describe and depict the diversity of features possessed by these streams would require a book of impractical thickness. The variety of animal life, plants, and geologic formations would fill scientific volumes. Ninety-five species of fish inhabit the two rivers, and thirty-nine species of rare and endangered plants can be found along the waterways. The natural history of the land includes everything from violent volcanic explosions of igneous rock, through inundations by a number of gentle seas, to eons of erosion during which the modern rivers set their courses.

The human history of this countryside is full of anecdote and upheaval as well. This is a land not always respected by men as it might have been, and the tale of man on the rivers is not always a proud one. Bushwhackers and murderers roamed the mountains during the Civil War; turn-of-the-century timbermen cut nearly every pine off the slopes until only bald knobs were left and the gravel was freed to tumble into the streams, choking them. Although they have proved remarkably resilient, the rivers are again under threat; this time the pressure is from the crush of the sheer numbers who come to enjoy them and who leave their indelible marks. All of this, past and present, is worth recording for the future.

To publish a book that draws attention and thereby more visitors to the rivers is an undertaking of some gravity. To show the beauty of the streams and then to provide artillery coordinates for the sites of special interest may be to sign a death notice for whatever solitude is left. It certainly makes the work something other than a celebratory ode to nature and charges it with a greater responsibility. For if it is the tangible subjects, not their interpretation and not some stylish first-person story about experiencing them, that are of value here, then how can a book that may in any way threaten those subjects be justified?

The authors found their solution to this quandary by always seeking to discover and present the reasons why this land and these rivers should be treated carefully and with respect. We have shown the light at play on the bluffs in the hope that no one who sees the photograph could again consider or tolerate the defacing of rock with paint. We have written about the natural history in an effort to offer a feeling, if not a step-by-step explanation, for those plodding forces that have crafted the mountains and the streams.

Fifty years of floating and fishing on these rivers have been instrumental in setting the approach of this book. With more to tell and show than space in which to do it, there has been no attempt to be encyclopedic. Instead, the design of *Two Ozark Rivers* is experiential. We began with those aspects of the rivers that have been important to us, with the questions we asked ourselves as we moved down the waterways. Many scenes of interest have been purposely left out. Volumes of information concerning the rivers have yet to be written. There is room for a reader's personal experiences to fill in the gaps and for the mysteries of flowing water to weave between the lines.

The forty-mile length of the Jacks Fork River, from where it begins at the junction of two creeks, called The Prongs, to its confluence with the Current, is here. The Current River is followed from its headwaters at Montauk Springs for a distance of ninety miles to Big Spring, by which time the river has undergone a change in character.

Much of the rivers' recent history revolves around the day in 1964 when a portion of their lengths was established as the nation's first federally protected scenic rivers by an act of Congress. That law calls for the protection of the "unique scenic and other natural values and objects of historical interest, including preservation of portions of the Current River and the Jacks Fork River in Missouri as free-flowing streams." To that worthwhile end the authors hope this book also contributes.

But since that day, the one hundred–plus square miles designated for protection have been colored green on every map, enticing vacationers in increasing numbers until, on some summer weekends, the visitor in search of a wilderness experience may well wonder if he hasn't found a canoe parking lot rather than a free-flowing stream.

There are, of course, other seasons besides summer and a wide assortment of activities and things to learn about. Perhaps *Two Ozark Rivers* will help some readers to find new ways to enjoy themselves without having to join a crowd. We hope that by representing what is available to see and do, we can refresh the memories of those who have visited the rivers while we whet the appetites and hone the sensitivities of those who have not yet found these wonderful places. By preparing the reader for some of the experiences to be had here, perhaps the book will engender a respect for the land and the water in our charge and under our collective stewardship.

For whether the land in the long run belongs to all of us or to none, man does have power over it at the moment and can choose what will become of it. Each of our visits to the wilds has an effect. If we all could become aware of that effect and careful with our own individual impacts in order that artificially induced change be kept to a minimum, the end result would be for the good. That is what *Two Ozark Rivers* is about.

Acknowledgments

The authors owe a great deal to the many people who worked so hard and contributed so much during the creation of *Two Ozark Rivers*. Our heartfelt thanks to all those who provided inspiration and guidance.

We are grateful to our old friends Ira and Myrtle Moss, and to their eldest son, Phillip, who ran the johnboat on those raw days. We deeply appreciate the kindness shown us by Alva and Bernice Bunch and by Roger and Betty Curry. We are also indebted to Patty Gabriel and to Ann Hoffman, teaching assistant and paddling companion, as well as to good friends Pete and Chips. Naturalists Leonard Hall and Ron Mullikin led by example, and we thank them. And, of course, much is due Peggy Kohler and Judy and Matthew Schuchard, without whom the authors would get nothing done. We are also indebted to our new friends, especially to Jere Krakow, Chris White, Alex Outlaw, and Jack Piepenbring at the park. They helped so much and they protect what we love.

Special thanks are reserved for those wise and skilled people who voluntarily read the text, made suggestions, and caught errors, by name, L. D. Brodsky, Art Hebrank, Leonard Hall, Jere Krakow, and Tim Renken.

Our work would have been impossible without the generous assistance of the Old Town Canoe Company of Old Town, Maine, manufacturers of the finest in paddle craft. Thanks also to Columbia Photo Supply of Columbia, Missouri, for all the help provided by the staff.

We would also like to thank Richard L. Wallace, Associate Dean for Research, and Frank H. Stack, Chairman of the Department of Art, both from the University of Missouri–Columbia, for their support of *Two Ozark Rivers*. Finally, the photographic documentation for this project was funded by a grant from the Research Council of the Graduate School, University of Missouri–Columbia.

Contents

Two Ozark Rivers

1.

Prologue

WERE the Current and the Jacks Fork somehow to do the impossible and become suddenly human, they would likely be hill country old-timers with a full charge of the wisdom that comes only with the years. They'd be pine-knot tough and indomitable and adventurous and spry, just like many of those people who have lived along their banks for generations.

They'd be lively grandparents whose twinkle and sharp patter are always a surprise. With a clear vision, an impertinence, and an honesty that remains long after parting, they would be the exceptional folks well remembered for having an especially bright spark of life, always crackling with energy.

Or they might be tight friends, with an engagingly simple manner, so dear because they always see things just differently enough to offer a fresh outlook or to reveal a curiously hidden way of thinking.

Of course, the Current and the Jacks Fork are not human. They are rivers, much rarer than people, and especially so because they are free flowing and relatively undisturbed. Yet they do possess some of the characteristics of living things, including the élan vital of these waterways, their potential for change.

On every scale, the rivers display a mutability that reveals their essence. Two very different streams will be encountered by the paddler who makes a pair of trips over the same route, even if only a few days elapse between floats. The change is always happening, whether or not witnesses are present to record it. These Ozark rivers have been here in all their fluidity and adaptability for sixty-five million years. They drain mountains that are among the earth's oldest, and they meandered across a vast plain in the age before the land was upthrust.

Throughout their existences, the Current and the Jacks Fork have altered themselves and been altered by natural forces. Courses have changed, forests have come down, gravel has washed, and floods have carved whole new channels. Islands have been born, and dirt has been hauled while entire civilizations and industries have flourished and died. These days, almost 2 million visitors annually have their collective hand on the throttle of accelerating change, with controversial and far-reaching repercussions.

Season to season, the streams initiate their cyclical changes, floating them in and carrying them away. Flowers along the bank foretell spring, blooming in the newly replenished soil before they appear anywhere else. The big floods, with their flat, tan color and the audible hiss of sand being borne along, often come in late winter to sweep out debris left by the erosive action of ice and snow. In summer, the sky seems its bluest over the water for its reflection from the shiny surface. And as that blue deepens to a shade that appears only in

A May panorama focuses on the old Chilton place, one of the first farms on the upper Current River and the former home of the Owl's Bend Stock Farm from which the sweep in the river draws its name.

When heavy rains double the discharge of Blue Spring, high water in the branch sweeps into a succession of standing waves.

At many places along the course of the streams, forest vegetation creeps right to the junction of land and water; the wealth of one realm feeds the other.

the autumn, the rivers become their most jewel-like, enhancing another season's leaves of gold, orange, and brown.

In the course of just one day, a careful watcher will note a striking change upon the water. From a bluff at dawn, the river looks gray and cold under blankets of mist. By ten o'clock the sun will have dispersed the cover, and what appeared to be a dead wrinkle in the earth will have become a shining blue stripe. Past noon, when the angle of light has progressed upstream, green will swathe everything in sight, and the river's emerald color will make even the leaves and the grass look flat and shallow by comparison. Let a storm blow in, though, and choppy waves will chatter on the water, gray again, with serious mountain weather arriving in alarmingly short order.

The rivers are lifelike, too, in their ability to exert an amiable attraction for other living things. White-tailed deer drink, little green herons feed, goggle-eye swim, and crawdads crawl along the bottom; life uses these rivers, shares them in many ways. Most human visitors feel that tug as well. Only a few leave without having experienced something of the rivers' attraction, their powers of influence. Only a few may fail to pick up an insight into life, because they don't allow the rivers time and a chance. Those who can't shed preconceived attitudes about the out-of-doors or who can't forget the pace of life back home may be the only ones not captivated, not enchanted.

This is a friendly wilderness, inviting and instructive. It is easy to get to, simple to get into, and pleasant to enjoy for long periods of time without hardship. The truths an unsullied environment has for us lie close to the surface in southern Missouri, all artifice having eroded away eons ago. The particular beauty on the Current and the Jacks Fork is not of the variety that immediately overwhelms; it creeps up on you rather than jamming your eyes open wide. The grace and restfulness of the Ozarks seep into you. Nature's style here runs to depth, not sizzle; to staying power, not flash.

We all go to the wilds for our own reasons, but tied up somewhere within most is the notion that our lives could be, should be, simpler. Whether hailing from a city hundreds of miles away or from Eminence just down the road, we intuit that if we can only escape telephones, television, and other irrelevant trappings of society, the hectic pressure will ease. Perhaps if we can just put some distance between ourselves and the nearest advertisement we will be able to slow down to a more natural pace, something akin to river speed. Then life, which has been civilized, computerized, and conventionalized, will flood back into our dormant instincts and our waylaid senses.

We go to the woods or the mountains to discover for ourselves a comfortable niche in the real order of things. There come instants of revelation when matter and form suddenly make gut-level sense: doubts fall away and self-trust is revitalized. The money in our pockets by which we have measured ourselves becomes insignificant in a world that fits neatly together and in which we at last feel included. Such experiences are rare. They won't be hurried or forced, and the devices and skills of daily life won't win them. In fact, it may be that only after much of what is societal artifice has been scrubbed away can they even be expected to occur. And when they do, they often last only briefly and almost always end too soon.

But the Current and the Jacks Fork will wash away the crust of unnecessary pretense and

From a trail overlooking Powder Mill on a September morning, the Current River awakes in a blanket of fog.

Eminence's Methodist Church on a bright, clear day.

A quiet pool on the Current River not far from Cave Spring makes a likely looking home for goggle-eye and the less common freshwater drum.

The blooms of the flowering dogwood, Missouri's official state tree and a prominent Ozark understory resident, decorate the depths of Courthouse Hollow. (Overleaf)

tension that accumulates within, floating moments of pure, relaxed quietude right up to you until they practically bump against your shins.

You will have to be out in the flow, however. These streams demand participation. No drive along a route full of scenic vistas will do. Besides, there is no such road. The only way to get a good look at these rivers is from right down on them. Once there, the details will captivate your attention first: the engrossing way the water laps at a gravel bar, never twice the same and not at all like waves on a beach; a cedar tree, seventy feet up the face of a bluff, sticking out into space at an impossible angle, anchored only in a five-pound pocket of earth trapped on a rocky lip; or tadpoles, minnows, hellgrammites, and other assorted fry all going about their inscrutable business in a shoal so clear it must be only a rippling surface suspended above a vacuum.

A fifteen-foot stretch of gravel bar is subject enough for a full afternoon's study. And when it's time to leave after what feels like a casual few minutes of observation, the visitor might realize he's been at it for several hours, transported completely out of clock time and into the realm of river time. Slow and unmeasured, river time is marked off only by the splash and chatter of a nearby riffle. It slips away more easily than the usual sort of time. It can't be owned, or invested expecting a return, or taken away from some other work that should be getting accomplished. River time comes only to those who are relaxed and prepared to let the rhythms and flow of a stream soak into their senses.

The simplest way to feel those rhythms is to climb onto the seat of a paddled boat. From that level you can feel the tug of the current, the urge in the flow that sets the pace and moves you along. When the hull breaks final contact with shorebound gravel and the bow swings downstream in a speedy arc, immediately the paddler becomes just one more nit swept along on the rush. Staying in the flow, steering, maintaining the proper balance and a quiet ease occupy muscles, nerves, and thought.

The choices facing the paddler are straightforward, the rewards and penalties instantaneous. Should the boat go to the left or to the right of that rootwad ahead? Decide now, because here it comes. Hesitate too long, change your mind too late, or simply fail to make the right move, and you may soon be swimming to retrieve cooler, lunch, and paddle. The boating here is rarely dangerous in any life-threatening sense. Neither stream approaches the turbulence of the Colorado, the Snake, or even the Buffalo. The challenge offered is more subtle: can you use the river's energy, steer well, read the water's clues, and exercise skill? Can you stay in harmony, fit in, travel in style?

A newcomer's first few trips will probably be spent trying too hard, struggling and haggling unnecessarily. It takes a while to relax and let the running water do most of the work. The river traveler must learn to accept the water's terms without qualification; the streams will not be made into something they are not. Coming to confront the forces or to battle nature in order to prove one's self against the rivers won't work. It's that simple. The rivers will remain indomitable, their powers of a higher order. Water rising to overtake a poorly chosen gravel bar campsite is frustratingly and absolutely irreversible. A canoe saddlebagged around a blowdown is irretrievable without the aid of a good-sized tractor. And without a little practice, beginning boaters bang back and forth, bank to bank, traveling three times as far as necessary on their trips downriver. The way a hull cleaves through the moving, shifting

Never twice the same, river-country sunsets are best viewed from ridgetop or across a broad vista. From the canyonlike stream courses, the bluffs block the late light.

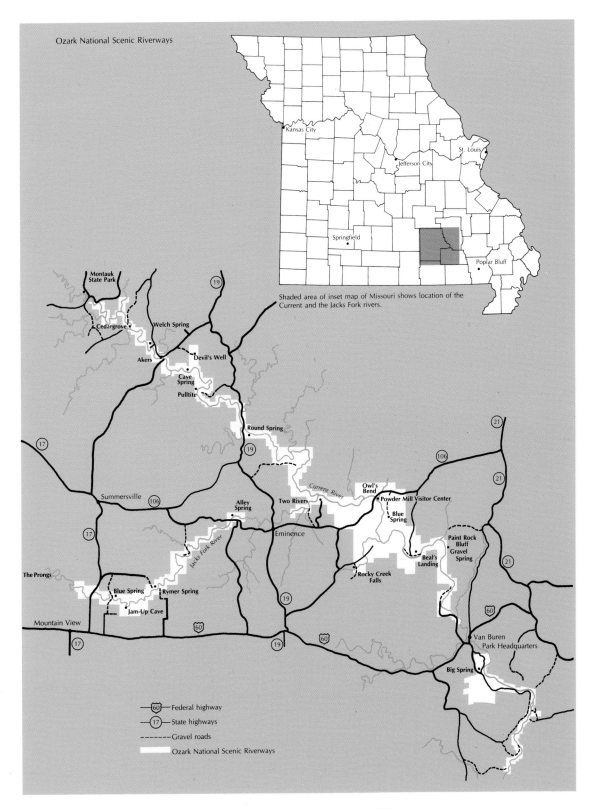

Ozark National Scenic Riverways

Montauk State Park
19
Cedargrove
Welch Spring
Akers
Devil's Well
Cave Spring
Pulltite
Round Spring
19
17
Summersville
106
Alley Spring
Two Rivers
Current River
Owl's Bend
Powder Mill Visitor Center
21
21
106
Blue Spring
17
Eminence
Jacks Fork River
Paint Rock Bluff Gravel Spring
21
The Prongs
Beal's Landing
Rocky Creek Falls
Blue Spring
Rymer Spring
Jam-Up Cave
Mountain View
19
60
60
Van Buren Park Headquarters
17
19
60
Big Spring

Kansas City
St. Louis
Jefferson City
Springfield
Poplar Bluff

Shaded area of inset map of Missouri shows location of the Current and the Jacks Fork rivers.

60 — Federal highway
17 — State highways
- - - - Gravel roads
▬▬▬ Ozark National Scenic Riverways

Summer's progression into fall is measured by the change of dogwood foliage.

13

Stacks of trailered canoes at Aker's Ferry await the season's floaters.

During a parched July, portions of the rivers that lie above the bigger springs are reduced to unnavigable trickles.

water is a complex shadow puzzle that takes experience to understand. The constantly changing surface and the unseen forces beneath must be experienced time after time, until their meanings register intuitively. Any simple set of rules for controlling a boat will fail as often as it succeeds.

While travel here is only perilous at high water levels, proper and expert paddling is tricky at all river stages. The skill required makes every trip an adventure, and even old hands are kept honest by the need to make midcourse corrections and adjustments. There is more than enough learning on the Current and the Jacks Fork to last a lifetime.

Come to the riverbank at age eight to set sticklike toy boats free on the downstream rush. Launched one after another, they sweep through eddies and tumble over falls in high adventure of the imagination. Watching minnows chase a trail of soggy crackers into a glass trap or practicing the fine art of skipping rocks fills the time between greasing up for sunburn protection and charring hot dogs over a driftwood fire.

By age fourteen, an urge to learn more about the rivers sets in and summer school goes into session in the mountains. The witty, sometimes brilliant names of Ozark places and things grab the fancy. Library books reveal that the word *Ozark* came down through history from the people with bows, or, in French *aux arcs*—the Osage Indians. Another source has it that the same tribe hunted with longbows crafted from the wood of the Osage orange tree, called the *Bois d'arc,* and that this French name has been rendered as *Ozark.* The Current River, also named by early French trappers, was originally called *La Riviere Courant,* the running river. Maps color in a dim vision of history, pointing out Wildcat Hollow at the base of Buzzard Mountain, and Stillhouse Hollow, Troublesome Hollow, and Pistol Barrel Hollow all on the same stretch of water. From local folks comes the knowledge that the Jacks Fork is named for Captain Jack, a Shawnee Indian chief who camped with his tribe along the riverbank near today's Big and Little Shawnee creeks. The disciple also soon learns there are no rapids on these rivers. Those places where the water runs quickly over the gravel are called shoals, riffles if the turbulence is a notch higher. When such spots pose problems in maneuvering a canoe or a johnboat down their lengths, they become chutes. But a solid understanding of the lay of the land—up which hollows the best springs lie, where two ridges intersect, and when a running deer will cross the river—would require a lifetime of study. And still, you'd come up short of a born riverman's natural savvy.

At eighteen, a young man's daydreams are populated by the men who live on the river, the old-timers who know instinctively where the big fish hide and who never go out into the sun without a hat. River time is filled with the intricacies of learning from them how to handle a boat: what to watch out for, where the deep water flows, and when to dip the paddle so only a few strokes will do for a mile or more of travel. Late at night, there are trotlines to be run away from the warmth of a gravel-bar blaze and frogs to be grabbed from a bank beneath the spooky blue mist, while owls put eerie question marks to the tales told by the whip-poor-wills.

Back to the water at twenty-five years old after too long away, it's easy to think how much like a lover the river is—unpredictable, yet calm, soothing, and essential. Showing off rusty skills to a partner, the urge to talk too much and tell what can only be experienced is hard to resist.

By the time you reach forty, the river has become such an integral part of you that it is difficult to speak of it at all. Idle conversation, like a dull snapshot in an album, doesn't capture any of the stream's real significance. Pleasure comes instead from showing others those cherished places, those times of day when everything is special to eye and ear, or the vantage points remembered for having provided startling revelations.

Often, with still more age and time spent on the water comes enough wisdom to see the playfulness embodied by the rivers. For all their lessons about order, form, and restraint, the streams also advise their old and initiated friends against taking them, or anything else, too seriously. After all, they are composed entirely of elements in constant change.

The Current and the Jacks Fork are inviting and open. A tutelage there may be undertaken no matter at what age or with what previous experience one comes to them. Once begun, a relationship with these two rivers is likely to grow.

An old smithy's shed houses a blacksmithing demonstration during the summer months at the Powder Mill Visitor Center.

2.

Watershed

SQUARELY in the middle of the country—equidistant from the Rockies and the Appala-chians—rise the Ozarks, the mountainous terrain that forms the watershed for the Current and Jacks Fork rivers. Old and rounded by time, the mountains owe much of their configuration to the streams that drain them, and the rocky roughness of their slopes provides a textural counterpoint to the lithesome, meandering rivers.

Purists argue that the Ozarks should not be called mountains, that Missouri elevations topping out at seventeen hundred feet are not lofty enough to qualify the region as a true mountain range. As alternatives they suggest referring to the area as Ozark highlands, Ozark uplift, plateau, dome, uplands, or hills.

From an airplane seat or a desk chair, the Ozarks may count only as hill country, but climb any of their steep inclines during August's dog days, when hickory branches reach out to snag the skin and the humidity sticks like a wet rag in the throat, and in the memory they will be mountains forever. Or stand on a bluff two hundred feet above the river to share the thermals with a soaring red-tailed hawk, and they are undoubtedly mountains of the first order. Arguments aside, perhaps the region is best referred to by the name used hereabouts: simply, the Ozarks. Anything more than that is restrictive, for this land is everything any name ever given it implies and more; these are mountains and then some.

The Ozarks have a long history, influenced in many ways by events over time. Whether the topic is the wealth of plant life and the many endemic species that survive hidden in the sinks and deep hollows, the welter of animal life that teems in the forest, or merely the weather, in each instance the fascinating thing about the Ozarks is how many diverse facets make up the whole gem, how different everything is at each bend in the river, at every turn in the trail.

Like a steamer trunk full of treasures discovered in an attic, the Ozark mountains are a collection of remembrances from the planet's past, a storehouse of nature's mementoes. Half a million years ago, when the Kansas glaciation crept southward to stop just short of leveling these mountains, northern plant species were forced ahead of the cold. Some of them survive today in the cool, damp environment of the spring branches. Relicts from a vast and ancient eastern hardwood forest persist in the Ozark woods. And on the glades, specimens continue to thrive from the time when the climate resembled modern Arizona's. To the north and east flow the continent's two largest rivers, making this a truly riverine setting. To the west lie the great prairies; to the southeast is the Mississippi embayment, up which seas came flooding time and again during geologic prehistory.

Mixed foliage dapples the bank with color along the face of the Blue Spring bluff.

A well-preserved example of the old Ozark one-room schoolhouse, Storys Creek School first saw students in 1896. Seventy-five years later, the schoolhouse was moved to Alley Spring to become a part of the National Park Service's interpretive history program.

From a ridgeline along the Ozark Trail, the view across the river valley is through hardwoods, cedars, and haze. (Overleaf)

To generalize about the land surrounding the rivers is risky; its variety and its many isolated pockets of individuality follow no broad rules. In these two rivers alone swim ninety-five species of fish. More than fifteen hundred plant varieties grow on bottomland, slope, and ridgetop, and forty-three mammalian species make their homes in the vicinity of the streams. Insects, aquatic and otherwise, abound in uncounted numbers. And bird-watchers prize the area for its additions to their lists of seldom-seen birds. The rivers contain no straight sections of any length, invariably wandering to turn in a new direction, to settle into a deep pool or hurry across a shoal. The land is rough and raw, ready to trip or gouge with a rock or a stub, and demanding of those who make their homes here.

On porches all across the region Ozarkers say the soil is so poor that to grow anything a farmer has to tie his seed between two rocks to keep it from blowing away; that it's impossible to raise even the windows without jacking up the house; that cows are tied together by the tails in pairs and set to graze on either side of the ridge so they don't roll downslope and drown in the rivers.

Ozark weather is so unpredictable that a certain resigned acceptance sets in among the hill folks whenever one of the many extremes is at hand. Flood, tornado, stifling heat, bone-numbing cold, three-foot snows, and twelve-inch rains, it's all the weather of home to an Ozarker. It may be a topic of conversation if conditions turn balmy in February or if it snows in September, but a staunch resolve still rules those who suffer such wild swings of climate. Coming in out of a downpour, soaked to the skin, an Ozarker is liable to ask, "Think it'll rain?" The common answer: "If it don't it's missin' a good chance." A six-month growing season, two hundred days of sun each year, and the thrill of the unexpected make up for whatever climatological hardships must be endured.

*   *   *

Spring is the wet weason in the watershed. As the cold of winter loosens its grip on the soil, a series of freezing and thawing spells sets in to release water that has been trapped. Then rains come to wash the already sodden ground, and every slope runs wet. Along the vertical bluff faces, water flows in sheets. Each seep becomes a spring, every cave home to its own stream. The rivers eventually catch every drip and rivulet, draining the watershed of its seasonal excess.

Fourteen inches of rain fall during March, April, and May, and much of the weather is highly localized. Storms frequently overpower one hollow while a mile away the sun shines on another. Such weather pockets cause creeks to rise unexpectedly and influence even larger rivers so that a jump in their levels has no immediately apparent source.

Running in rocky, bluff-bound valleys without room to spread out, the Current and the Jacks Fork rise quickly. The river bottoms of both streams are prone to flash flooding. On April 30, 1983, a single day's hard rain fell upon ground that had been saturated for several weeks, bringing both rivers up dramatically to levels recorded only once every fifty years or so. Eyewitnesses to the flood on the upper Jacks Fork reported that at 4:00 P.M. the river carried five feet of water. At the flood's crest six hours later, the same spot was marked at thirty feet.

Such floods do damage largely to man's additions to the natural landscape and are self-limiting, serving several positive purposes. High water hauls away nature's accumulations,

Evening storm clouds clear from the sky above the Jacks Fork, reflecting the last, warm rays of the sun.

Late winter's heavy, wet snow clings firmly to trunk and branch.

moves gravel out of shallowing stream channels, deposits new and richer riverbank soil, and removes weak trees from the bankline to make way for the new.

Major floods often, though not always, arrive in late winter or early spring when precipitation is frontal. Then, the dry, cool air of the north collides with moisture-laden, summery masses pushing up from the Gulf of Mexico. But spring's generally low humidity levels spawn thin, bright days that offer a period of delightful relief between the chill of winter and the sodden, weighty air of deep summer. Frost still settles in mid-April, and even a week or two later in the hollows where protection is afforded the cool air that slips off the ridges.

Use of the rivers by recreational canoeists doesn't begin in earnest until after Memorial Day has passed, so an early spring float trip is a pleasantly quiet one full of the sights and sounds of an awakening countryside. Winds invariably gust into the face of the early-season boater just as he attempts to steer his craft, and sometimes not even the warmth of a campfire can eliminate the chill of a cold rainshower. A floater is lucky to string together more than two perfect days during March or early April. But the small risks are worth the rewards of solitude and adventure to be found during the warming days and crisp nights.

＊　　＊　　＊

Spring is also the time of year when the multitude of plants and animals that inhabit the watershed return to life from dormancy. The greening up begins deep in winter and reaches a peak of yellowy brilliance as April becomes May. Lengthening daylight hours and building warmth stir creatures to action.

More than 80 percent of the land in the counties through which the Current and the Jacks Fork flow is covered in forest and wild vegetation. In addition to those obvious residents that this vast woodland supports—the wildflowers and trees, the squirrels and deer—the forest's abundance figures into other, less visible realms. Insects and nits and microbial life of every description wash downslope into the waterways from the rich and organically active floor of the woods. That abundant food supply, combined with the pool-riffle-pool configuration of the rivers, the water's high oxygen content, and an ample supply of cover, make the streams a near-perfect habitat for fish that vary in size from full-grown minnows less than an inch long to tall-tale catfish of legendary weight.

The largest of all fish families is made up of minnows. Fifteen hundred species are known worldwide, and twenty-two have been recorded in the two rivers. Most are small and many are brilliantly colored, including the bleeding shiner that displays a bright red splash on head, fins, and sides during the spawning season of May and June. Like many fish here, the bleeding shiner depends upon the gravel bottoms in the streams for a spawning bed to protect its eggs. And like twelve other species, this minnow has so adapted to life in the cool, clear flow of the Current and the Jacks Fork that it appears nowhere else.

Fish continue to grow as long as they live, a thought that delights the hearts of those who angle for the smallmouth bass, king of Ozark sportfish. Colored remarkably like the background of its habitat, the smallmouth feeds by sight, pursuing only moving objects that it ambushes with a vengeance. The smallmouth, or brownie, occupies flowing water over a

The dense forest vegetation closes in, giving the impression that the river runs in a leafy canyon.

Igneous rock dating from Precambrian times breaks through a bed of sand on the Indian Creek bottoms.

A broad beech fern, common to rich, forested hollows, flashes yellowy green in the damp lushness of streamside.

clean gravel bottom and may make its lifelong home in one pool of the river no more than a half-mile in length. Averaging growth of three inches per year, a ten-inch smallmouth weighs about one-half pound. After six years, a healthy brownie approaches five pounds in weight, something many fishermen dream of.

But the biggest of the resident game fish is the channel catfish, which regularly attains a weight of fifteen pounds. White, flaky meat and a temperament that prevents it from being easily landed make the chucklehead, as the fish is also known, a much-sought quarry. Channel cats feed by taste and have a well-developed sense of hearing. Night feeders, they work the deep, slow pools and are most often taken on trotlines checked from a boat every few hours. Between trips to run the line, bottled warmth keeps the fishermen's conversation flowing around a gravel-bar campfire, in the custom of time-honored Ozark sport.

A sure sign that winter is gone from the rivers is the sight of turtles taking the sun on riverbank blowdowns. The yellow-marked cooter and the somewhat smaller midland smooth softshell, two species that abound, can be seen relaxing wherever there's a sunny log. The softshell is a game animal in Missouri, and its pursuers claim to find seven different kinds of meat on the turtle, each more delicious than the last. A more secretive indigenous reptile is the alligator snapper. Rare, protected by law, and formidable, the snapper has changed little during 200 million years of existence and may reach a weight of 150 pounds, making it the largest freshwater turtle on earth. Snappers thrive on fish lured to a sharply hooked beak by a wormlike tongue.

Draped casually among the same roots on which turtles gather is likely to be another ancient specimen, the copperhead, one of five poisonous snakes native to Missouri (the others are the cottonmouth, or water moccasin, and three species of rattlesnake). Less shy than most snakes, copperheads are identifiable by their gray-brown skin marked with a double-diamond pattern of a darker hue. Not aggressive unless threatened, the copperhead is best left undisturbed. The black ratsnake, or black snake, is a still more common resident of the watershed. Startlingly long at six feet and beyond, the black snake frequents old farm buildings and streamsides. Displaying the musculature of a constrictor, it is able to climb trees and can stand against a vertical wall with only a tail-end inch or two on the horizontal. Harmless to humans and beneficial especially to farmers, the black snake has a big appetite for rodents.

Near the riverbanks, where rich, alluvial soils may accumulate to depths of six feet, grow the water-loving plant species. Standing on the floodplain are green ash, a shade tree of strong, hard wood; red and silver maples, so illusively plain in spring and summer but brilliant in fall's reds and yellows; and American sycamores, called the ghost of the woods for their white, scaly bark that seems to glow when struck by moonlight. Sycamores here are huge trees, larger than any others in the forest. In the spring, their seeds can be seen afloat on the river, each with its own tuft of hair for buoyancy in the air and on the water.

Other species adopt the same ploy for spreading their kin, using the streams as avenues of transportation. On the gravel bars shifted by each season's high water, sandbar willows sprout from seeds left by the tide, their roots holding new deposits in place against the force of the water. Other species common to the gravel bar include Ozark witch hazel—thought to have medicinal powers, especially for rashes of the skin—water willow, and black willow. Witch hazel branches are highly regarded by dowsers, or water witches, as the best tools for use in the search for sources of subterranean water.

The watershed supports a colorful array of flora.

Away from the bank only a short distance grows the American hornbeam, a small understory tree also known as musclewood for its extremely hard wood and its fluted trunk that resembles well-developed sinew. Beside the hornbeam flourishes the sassafras, another usually small tree that thrives in fertile soil and may attain heights of sixty feet at river's edge. The bark and twigs of the sassafras have long been brewed into a spring tonic and cooked to produce candy, jelly, tea, or a medicine to combat fever. Separate male and female plants exist, though both bear the tree's three distinctive leaf shapes. The wood of the sassafras makes strong posts and is employed in boat building for its resistance to rot.

Water-loving wildflowers native to the bottomlands include the fiery cardinal flower (*Lobelia cardinalis*), abloom from July to October; the dog-tooth violet (*Erythronium albidum*), or trout lily, a true lily rising from a bulb; and the bloodroot (*Sanguinaria canadensis*), with its single, stark white bloom that lasts only a day. Long ago, the root of this wildflower provided a source of dye for the native Osage Indian population.

Among the most prized Ozark wildflowers is the goldenseal (*Hydrastis canadensis*), little brother of ginseng, said to have power as a tonic and a panacea for everything from drowsiness to the effects of old age. Goldenseal is known by its hairy stalk, distinctive deep-green leaves, and a lone white flower in the spring. In the fall, it bears a cluster of red berries. Sometimes called Indian iceroot, goldenseal is threatened by poachers who profit by selling the medicinally important wild roots. Any colony of plants discovered should be left undisturbed.

Amid the tangle of plants taking advantage of the bottomland's plenty lives the raccoon. With an appetite for a wide variety of foods, 'coons leave their tracks on the riverbank wherever there is mud or sand to hold them. Curious and busy, they reach an average weight of twenty pounds, though the males, boars, are often larger. In late fall, hunters gather at night with their hounds to pursue raccoons through the hills. Whether redbone, treeing walker, or blue tick, the coonhound is a distinguishing part of the Ozark countryside, possessed of a lazy-looking style and a heart on fire to run in the woods.

Joining the 'coon on the riverbank is the beaver. At up to sixty pounds and four feet in length, the beaver is the biggest rodent on the continent. Able to spend as much as fifteen minutes underwater at a time, this critter possesses huge rear feet for power in swimming, nostrils mounted on the side of its nose that close for diving, and an oil-producing gland for the waterproofing of its own fur—all in all, a masterpiece of design in an aquatic mammal. Prized for its pelt since the days of the early French trappers, the once threatened beaver has rebounded until it is again widespread in the Ozarks. Today, long stretches of bank are sometimes stripped of the saplings that provide the beavers' food. Unable to tame the swift waters of the Current and the Jacks Fork, beavers here forego their well-known habit of damming streams to settle instead for homes dug into the bankside.

Upslope, in the forest proper, the limbs of the dominant oak and hickory trees are home to fox and gray squirrels—gnawing rodents like the beaver. Graced with bushy tails they use for shade, balance, and blanketlike warmth, as well as for umbrellas in the rain, squirrels are the woods' most common mammals. As rare in the Ozarks as the squirrel is common, the bobcat is not often seen thanks to its solitary nature. This yard-long cat with tufted ears and only a stub of a tail can sometimes be heard, however, near dusk when it issues its piercing scream of a cry. A consummate carnivore, the bobcat's numbers have been greatly reduced by its sensitivity to decreasing habitat and other pressures of man. Nevertheless, the secretive cat can survive undetected in areas where it has long been thought to have been forced out.

The specific mixture of trees through which such woodland animals move has long been interpreted by Ozarkers as an indicator of soil quality. Where healthy hickories and white oaks thrive, farmers prize the soil. A stand of red oak indicates less fertile but still valuable ground, and where post oaks grow, farmers have little luck. Native shortleaf pines and blackjack oaks will flourish on a plot without enough soil to support even a crop of grass.

Sheltered beneath the pine and hardwood canopy of the forest, many other species thrive. One of the most common understory trees of the hillslope is Missouri's official tree, the flowering dogwood (*Cornus florida*). Spreading its branches in broad, horizontal sweeps, the dogwood blooms about the first of May and turns the woods white with a profusion of blossoms that may each surpass the size of a silver dollar. The four white parts of the bloom that appear to be petals are actually modified leaves that open to reveal the less spectacular true flower. In the fall, dogwoods shine a second time when they carry many bright red berrylike drupes. The dense wood of the dogwood tree is used for golf club heads and mallets and in other applications requiring a resistance to shock.

Where the dogwood blooms can also be found the mayapple (*Podophyllum peltatum*), a wildflower sometimes called mandrake, which, in its namesake month, sprouts one or two large leaves that droop to conceal first a lone white bloom and later an edible fruit. Other parts of the plant are poisonous. The forest floor here is also home to the trillium (*Trillium sessile*), or wake-robin, a three-leaved plant that bears a three-petaled purple or deep red flower. One of Missouri's most beloved wildflowers, the trillium has been adopted as the symbol of the state's natural areas. Another favorite, columbine (*Aquilegia canadensis*), springs in clusters from pockets of earth trapped on the faces of bluffs. Blooming in five telltale spurs, this delicate-looking but hardy plant's flower changes in shade from yellow at the bottom, through rose, to red at the tip.

As surprising and beautiful as they are, even wildflowers have among their numbers the mean-spirited few. In the Ozark watersheds, the worst of the lot is poison ivy (*Rhus radicans*). Found in many settings growing to heights of ten feet, it is a relative of both the pistachio nut and the deceptively similar but nonirritating sumac that turns flame red at the first hint of fall weather. Poison ivy blooms in small, yellow flowers during May and June, and it carries white, waxy berries in autumn. The sticky, irritating oil exuded from leaves, stems, and roots has an effective life of more than a year after the plant has died.

Deer are apparently immune to the effects of poison ivy and seek it out as a favorite food. The largest mammal common to the Ozarks, the white-tailed deer is well outfitted for its life in the mountains. Capable of speeds to thirty miles per hour on the hoof, an accomplished swimmer with buoyant, insulating, and hollow hairs in its winter coat, the deer is also able to hide in plain sight, and sometimes survives to an age of fifteen years. A deer can leap a six-foot fence from a standstill and move with uncanny silence through a dry and brittle autumn woods. The white-tail is a descendant of animals that migrated across a land bridge from Asia 15 million years ago. Adapting to climatic changes and the pressures of man, the seemingly fragile deer has established itself as a survivor. Today, the Missouri Department of

Daisies claim an abandoned pasture on the Current River's rich upper reaches. (Overleaf)

Conservation protects white-tails from the twin threats of habitat encroachment and the success of hunters, whose numbers are monitored and licensed.

Interspersed among the dense cover where deer and other woodland animals dwell are a few prairielike, dry, and open places—separate environments with their own isolated plant populations. These Ozark glades are remnants of the arid climate that prevailed during the late Tertiary period. The underlying dolomite or limestone is often exposed on the glades, which are called balds when they occur on the narrow ridgetops that characterize the landscape. Missouri's only cactus, the prickly pear (*Opuntia compressa*), blooms in many bright yellow flowers on such limestone flats. Accompanying its roselike blossom are the fragrant flowers of the Missouri evening primrose (*Oenothera missouriensis*), the prolific black-eyed Susans (*Rudbeckia hirta*), and the succulent rock pinks (*Talinum parviflorum*). Only a rare, tough tree invades this harsh environment of a few inches of black, loamy soil that is soaked to sogginess in spring and baked to concrete in summer. Most common is the Eastern red cedar, known by its red, aromatic heartwood and blue-white berries.

Also surviving on the glades is the persimmon. A small tree sheathed in blocky bark, the persimmon bears a one-inch berry that ripens to a frosted orange color and a wrinkled appearance in the fall. Eaten too early, persimmons will make your mouth pucker; sometimes they are astringent to the point of pain. When ripe, they make a delicious beer, pudding, marmalade, or pie. For a taste of this wild fruit, gather soft, ripe persimmons and try some persimmon bread. Mix two cups of white cornmeal; one cup of crushed, ripe persimmons with the seeds removed; one-half teaspoon baking soda; one-half teaspoon baking powder; one-half cup milk; one egg; a dash of cinnamon; and a dash of salt. Thin the mixture if necessary and bake as you would corn bread for twenty to twenty-five minutes in a 450-degree oven in a well-seasoned, black cast iron skillet with plenty of preheated drippings.

In order to round up the succulent persimmons required for cooking, you'll have to be energetic. A favorite food of many woodland animals, the fruit disappears quickly once it begins to ripen. Birds, raccoons, and deer enjoy the delicacy, but it is the opossum that probably gets more than its share. The only North American marsupial, the 'possum is a strange, ugly, and ratlike rascal of the night that promptly feigns death when threatened with becoming a meal for an enemy, yet eats almost anything itself, including barnyard chickens. With a grasping tail and an opposable big toe, the 'possum's range in the forest is unrestricted.

As well suited as many Ozark critters are for their life in the woods, it is the great horned owl that holds down the top spot on the list of successful animals. This nocturnal raptor hunts and eats rabbits, mice, skunks, other birds, and a wide variety of similar prey. The great horned owl, known as "old eight hooter" for its evening call of eight notes that echo eerily off the bluffs, can sail between trees spaced more closely together than the span of its wings. It bears specially adapted wing feathers that allow perfectly silent flight. Tufts at the ears provide a basis for the name. The most voracious hunter in the woods, this great bird is granted many fantastic powers in folklore. Ozarkers warn against venturing into the forest at night while wearing a coonskin cap for fear that a hunting owl might mistake the hat for its quarry and sail silently into the back of the skull, talons first, with breakneck force.

The wild turkey, an even larger resident bird, has made a remarkable recovery after having been hunted and pressured into near extinction. Now present in healthy numbers thanks to

Many species of raptors can be identified by the careful watcher from the rivers. (Clockwise, from top left: bald eagle, barn owl, great horned owl, barred owl)

the state's management programs and game laws, wild turkeys are again hunted in two seasons. As the wiliest of all North American game animals, turkeys escape the average hunter six out of every seven years. Aided by extremely keen eyesight and hearing, the wild turkey takes alarm at even the slightest movement in the woods and warns other members of the flock through an involved system of communications.

Of all the animals of the watershed, the one most closely associated with the Ozarks in legend and character is the mysterious whip-poor-will. Active at dusk and on into the night, the whip-poor-will is related to the larger chuck-will's-widow and the nighthawk, all members of the goatsucker family that displays an ability to take insects on the wing. The whip-poor-will has been assigned folkloric powers as a magician and a god of the night. It is said to be a predictor of the future, a grantor of wishes made on the first call heard in the spring, and the rascal responsible for having transformed a frog into the moon. Another Ozark tale accuses this chunky little bird of portending a death in the home near which it calls. In a more optimistic story, it is said that a listener who shouts at the bird upon hearing the first call of the evening can predict the length of his own life by noting the number of times the bird continues to call after being yelled at. No omen could be more encouraging, since the whip-poor-will has been known to call more than a thousand times, nonstop. Should boredom or aggravation set in at the repetitiveness of this night cry, it is good to remember one of the ten commandments of Ozark life: "Thou shalt not curse the whip-poor-will; he sings for a brighter day tomorrow."

*   *   *

Summer in the Ozarks is both the best, easiest season and the worst, most uncomfortable season. Swimming in the chilly stream beneath a baking sun is a refreshing and lazy way to enjoy life. Only a few yards into the woods, however, and even the slightest exertion draws a perspiration that won't evaporate into the saturated air.

Climatologists categorize the weather in the Ozarks as either humid-continental or humid-subtropical, agreeing at least on the humid part. With relative humidities commonly at the 75 percent mark and average temperatures for June, July, and August that run at ninety degrees for a high and sixty-five for a low, summer often feels like a steam towel twisted around the nerves if the relief of the rivers is not available. A summer-long blue haze hangs between the mountains, visible from every overlook. One hill story claims that on the most intense days of summer, the lizards all carry white oak chips in their mouths wherever they go. The reason: should they ever want to sit down, they will need something to put under their tails for insulation from the scorching ground.

Only light winds blow in sunny summer, with breezes especially rare after sunset. On those common days when the mercury tops one hundred in the afternoon and the nighttime low doesn't drop below eighty, sleep can be hard to find in a damp bed. On the riverbanks and in the deep hollows, however, relief is available; there the cool air settles at night, spreading comfort. With the descent of darkness comes a damp fog that may hang over the lowlands until nine or ten the next morning. Residents of the bottoms claim the mist gets so

Near the headwaters of the Current River, bales of hay dot a farmer's fields.

thick they have to wear mosquito netting over their heads when they go out early, just to keep tadpoles out of their eyes.

Any time after early July, an unbroken string of fourteen to twenty-one blisteringly dry days is not unusual. Such droughts shrivel Ozark gardens and fields and turn the woods jagged and unfriendly. When a portion of the eleven inches of rain common to the summer months does arrive, it is usually as a squall-line storm, violent and brief. Such cloudbursts often pack hail, high winds, and brilliant lightning displays with rains that pound down onto a packed earth only to run off quickly, posing a threat of flash flooding. When weather fronts snap a week or more of sultry heat, there commonly follow a few days of puffy white cumulus clouds, deep blue skies, cooler temperatures, and lower humidities, all of which tempt the imagination with thoughts of autumn to come.

*   *   *

Autumn in the hills begins in September, although it opens hot, oppressive, and August-like, with only brief, interwoven stretches of the crisper weather to come. Rains become more frequent and longer in duration as the weather's characteristic changeability returns. By October, the skies have shed their haze and turned the deepest blue of the year. Thinner air blows more vigorously through the woods, and the atmosphere again becomes refreshing. Color delights the eye. Frost begins to settle into the hollows in October, arriving there several weeks before it first grazes the ridgelands.

As the trees take their signal from the shortening days and begin the change that will light the hills for weeks to come, Indian Summer, the Ozarks' finest outdoor season, intervenes. Brightly colored leaves, low humidities, warm days, and nights that cool sharply make Indian Summer long anticipated and all too short when, after only a week or two, it passes into the winter side of autumn.

By November, the second rainiest season of the year bears down, and occasional snow flurries swirl in the ever-sharper wind. Clouds settle into the hollows and river valleys; they haunt the hills and sweep upstream, passing undisturbed through the trees. For days at a time the tops of the mountains disappear into the mist. Wet weather becomes less violent but more common, and freezing and thawing alternate to make a slippery, sticky quagmire of the clay mud. Somehow, the rivers read the change and lose their shimmer, adopting a duller shade for the winter ahead. The last of the migratory birds depart the waterways for the warmer south. To replace them, bald eagles arrive from Saskatchewan. Fishing along the rivers for a few months, the eagles winter here before returning to their nesting sites.

*   *   *

There hasn't always been such a variety of seasons in the mountains. Sometime around 4 million years ago, give or take a half-million years, the climate in the region resembled that of a southwestern desert. And before that, back at the dawn of the planet's development, when all the ecosystem's water was in the form of vapor and the earth's fiery geologic forces

The calm waters of Round Spring flood a circular pool with blue to reflect the image of trees growing on the bluff above.

were violently active, back some 1.5 billion years, volcanic activity rocked the Ozark region.

Amazingly, igneous rock formed in those primeval eruptions is visible today in the watershed of the Current and the Jacks Fork. There are locations at which it is possible to stand on a knob of rock more than 1 billion years old. Few places provide a glimpse of such ancient underlayment. Among the volcanic rocks is dark red rhyolite that cooled fast in an exposed lava flow, solidifying to a glassy hardness that fractures cleanly along a face of extreme smoothness. Nearby can be found the related but more coarsely grained granite that cooled slowly beneath the planet's surface and condensed to such a hardness that even eons of weathering have done little more than take the edges off, sometimes rounding boulders into huge spheres. Among the oldest rock exposed anywhere, these two varieties can be seen where the processes of erosion have cut down through the overlying deposits.

The primordial igneous activity that occurred during the Precambrian era was followed by long erosion, and later by the invasion of the Cambrian oceans. Sweeping up from what is now the Gulf of Mexico came the seas, swirling around the worn, igneous peaks and flooding the valleys. Slowly, particulates in the water settled, marine organisms by the millions gave up their tiny skeletons, algal reefs grew and silicified, and the land sank beneath the tremendous weight of the water pushing down over the ages. The seas, each with a different composition, swept in and out, leaving behind the strata we can identify today. From the Upper Cambrian of 550 million years ago through the Ordovician age of 465 million years ago, the midcontinent was inundated by vast oceans that sometimes covered even the highest igneous peaks and sometimes left them protruding from the surface like isolated islands. It is believed that the region evolved to become desertlike following the recession of the Ordovician seas, and a deposit of windblown sand was laid down atop the earlier sedimentations.

Then more and more seas advanced, slowly, to drop their loads of dolomite and limestone. By the time the Mississippian period of geologic prehistory closed some 320 million years ago, most of the oceans' work was complete. Among their legacies are deposits of dolomite and other sedimentary rocks that run to two thousand feet in thickness. Not far from Two Rivers, where the Current and the Jacks Fork join, is an age-old igneous knob, the summit of one of the original volcanic peaks freed of its sedimentary mantle by erosion. Standing there, it is possible to look out over what appears to be just a shallow Ozark valley. In fact, the dolomite that settled into that early mountain valley may be hundreds of feet deep, having been deposited in layers by the primeval seas. The "side" of the igneous mountain on which the observer stands slopes away invisibily beneath the inlay of sedimentation.

Another of the enduring gifts left by the venerable oceans is the omnipresent chert, or flint, as it is known locally. A sedimentary rock, flint was deposited in beds and huge masses among the other calcareous sedimentation. Much harder than other sedimentary stone, harder in fact than glass, it is the gravel of the stream bottoms that helps to make the Ozark waterways so unlike any others. Serving as a trap for dirt, chert gravel maintains the clarity of the rivers that is their hallmark. It also works to retard the wholesale erosion of the slopes into the streams by forming an armorlike shell of flat, interlocking plates on the surface of the soil. Chert is finely textured, quartz based, and appears in colors ranging from pure white through reds and blues to black. It is the flint of Indian arrowheads and the stuff of every gravel bar, responsible like so many other details for its own portion of the character of the Current and the Jacks Fork. Some say flint even has value in the Ozark garden, where it keeps the vegetables—like the streams—from getting dirty.

In addition to many inundations, the Ozarks have undergone a series of uplifts throughout their history. Beginning with what was believed to be the major doming of the land approximately 380 million years ago, there have been several subsequent mountain-building events. Geologists do not agree on the causes for the upheavals, but it is believed that for a period of perhaps 60 million years following the first cataclysmic uplift, the Ozarks were subjected to the unremitting powers of erosion. Draining water, falling water, and wind slowly took the mountains down, rounding them and finally reducing them to a peneplain, or near plain. Evidence to support this theory of a long period of undisturbed erosion and plain making can be found in the nearly identical heights of the modern summits; the presence of rounded river gravel on upland flats; and the shut-in sections of some tributary creeks, where the waters have carved narrow channels into even the extremely resistant igneous rock beneath the softer sedimentary layers.

But the most apparent remnant of the old plain is the pattern of the streams' channels. When the flow of the rivers on the developing plain became sluggish for lack of relief, the streams began to meander. Their courses wandered in loops across the flats, searching for even the most minimal drop in elevation, much as prairie rivers do today. Slowly, those ancient streams etched their paths down into the surface.

Some 65 million years ago there came another in the series of uplifts. The land was raised, and the streams were rejuvenated to flow vigorously as mountain rivers again, running through countryside with renewed and substantial relief. But the river channels were already well established, and they remained in their entrenched courses. Thus today, the Ozark rivers are unusual for a wandering character combined with relatively high energy and considerable drops in elevation of as much as ten feet per mile. Such rivers are called antecedent streams because they are antecedent to, or older than, the surrounding uplift.

The recent mountain-building events were uneven pieces of work, with southern Missouri and parts of adjoining states uplifted to varying degrees. Differences in the hardness of the rock and uneven erosive forces have added to the relief in the hills as the streams have cut their courses ever more deeply into the valleys. Though the Boston Mountains to the southwest and the St. Francois Range to the northeast are home to peaks of greater elevations, nowhere within the boundary of the Ozark dome is the country more rugged and precipitous than near the Current and the Jacks Fork.

* * *

Although by comparative standards winter in the Ozarks is a milder season than summer, only the cold months demand serious preparation. Most of the weather lore developed during decades of experience in the hills relates to predicting the winter ahead, and the work required to cut, split, and stack enough firewood for the cold season is substantial.

Considerably less than a fourth of the mountains' yearly forty-five inches of precipitation falls during December, January, and February, but when it comes it arrives as sleet, freezing rain, and snow. Almost every winter harbors at least one damaging ice storm, and the average is three major snows per season. Total snowfall ranges between eight and sixteen inches, and the ground is customarily white for about twenty days.

Humidity, which is always a factor in Missouri weather, season aside, runs at a wintertime average of 70 percent, making the air feel colder than it actually is. The lowest temperatures to expect with any regularity in the hills are near minus ten degrees; winter's highs average forty-two, lows twenty-one.

Such cut-and-dried figures must always be taken as long-term averages only, with many extremes factored in. They hold true and offer comfort only until a blue ice storm carrying twenty inches of snow howls in from the northwest one night, and the temperature drops below zero and doesn't rise above for a week, while the wind screams day and night. Such an event can occur anytime from November through March.

The deep hollows and the relatively constant temperatures of the rivers have a softening effect on the winter weather, however, keeping it slightly less severe than in the surrounding flatlands. Protection is offered by the hills and held by the hollows. The ridges and valleys also create many microclimates even during socked-in winter. Deep hollows and north slopes protect patches of snow from the sun for weeks after all signs of the latest storm are gone from other locations. The rivers rarely freeze, due to their comparatively warm sources and brisk flow, but ice decorates the banks for much of the winter. In the spring hollows, where fifty-eight-degree water meets zero-degree air, winter is a season of constant condensation. A thick mist boils off the surface of the branches and hangs low, imbuing the atmosphere with an eerie density. Mountain roads, which follow ridgetops and dip into valleys only at stream crossings, become treacherous and often impassable during the storms of winter.

Wherever and whenever winter takes hold in the Ozarks, silence dominates. Cold and snow slow all activity and suck the noise from the hills. River traffic is at an absolute minimum during the frozen months, and the reduction in pressure on deer, raccoon, and many other species brings them to the fields and streambanks in search of food. Ozarkers spend a larger portion of their time indoors by the woodstove during the winter, regaling one another with tales of times when the weather got so cold that the coffee in their cups froze fast, so fast that the ice was still hot.

The output of Medlock Spring rushes from a collapsed cave, then sneaks between mossy boulders. A living cave opens into the subterranean world on the hillslope just above the spring outlet, around a bend upstream from Welch.

3.

Sources

IN the same way that an Ozark river acquires individuality and character, becoming more than just fluid running in a gravelly ditch, each of the springs that feeds the Current and the Jacks Fork is itself something greater than simply a spot at which water pumps out onto the ground.

Each spring has its own identity; many sit in remarkable and startlingly beautiful settings. Every one has a particular rate of flow, a distinct source of supply, and a long history. Though they all pour out the same water and their pools all reflect an identical sky, the blue color of no two springs is alike, their individual shades as private and inimitable as signatures. Many tumble from outlet to river down a branch lush with watercress and moss-softened rocks. And the spring hollows' green and temperate environments make them the pleasant home of many otherwise uncommon wildflowers.

Combine all the physical attributes of an Ozark spring, add in exact descriptions and measurements, and still missing would be the mystery and the surprise that are its essence. These places where liquid bursts from solid have long been associated with nonscientific, unquantifiable properties. In folklore they are the centers of healing and the revitalization of the soul, of community and rekindled friendship, of nature's wealth and her capacity for goodness.

Few places offer so intimate a look at profound natural workings. Nowhere else is such a primary connection with the environment more encouraged. The mystic force that springs exert drives almost every visitor to dip a hand or a toe into the waters for a closer sense of communion. Simply viewing them, even studying the hydrogeology involved, won't satisfy the urge they stir to become a part of them.

And springs are mysterious because they seem so happily impossible. Winter and summer, year after year, they change little, always maintaining a nearly constant temperature, almost universally clear and sparkling. Where can all the water possibly come from? How is it that such a flood can travel underground, completely hidden from sight and totally unknown? Full of mystery and yet so dependable, springs have the same humbling effect on thought as does a starry country sky on a crisp October night or the sea when it slams itself against the cliffs; they force us to realize there exists so much more beyond just the "me" of the moment.

We imagine things emerging from the earth as hot and thick, lavalike, or stony. But here is cool water in superabundance, water that commonly comes from above. Adding to a spring's otherworldliness is its water's spectral color, so clear but with a frosty tint that's remindful of the haze that hangs in the Ozark hollows all summer long.

Deep within Round Spring Caverns, calcite draperies left by slow-moving water adorn the room known as the tobacco barn.

Because they are singular, we think of springs as entities, as spots or places. Despite their clear water we can't see very far down into them, and so they are isolated. But back under the bluff and down the shaft through which the water runs, back out of the light where things get really spooky, is a whole system of caverns and conduits, tubes and tunnels carrying water, lots of water. These places we encounter where that water pours out over the ground are more correctly thought of as rips or flaws in the system than as the reason for it.

Well beneath the surface, water branches out in many directions through rock that has fractured and dissolved during half a billion years. This honeycombed reservoir is vast, storing immense quantities in the manner of a sponge. No matter where in these watersheds one goes, it is impossible to move very far from a spring or a cave. Caves are a part of the maze-work too, because a cavern is just an abandoned portion of the spring system here.

As complex and tortured as the surface topography is, with its undulating ridges and its twisting streambeds, the subterranean network is even more convoluted. The underground flow of water occurs at many levels, largely following joints, cracks, and bedding planes in the rock. This flow sometimes cuts a path deep beneath a surface waterway without any interaction of the two streams. It runs without regard for what surface dwellers call "downhill." The subterranean water courses and seeps through the rock following the fracture patterns until a conduit opens to the surface to release the flow into another realm.

The Ozark Plateau is regarded as among the nation's regions richest in both caves and springs, and one of the highest concentrations of these features in the Ozarks is along the banks of the Current and the Jacks Fork. At least fifty picturesque springs of all sizes and in a wide variety of settings line the two rivers and their tributaries. In addition, almost 3,000 of Missouri's 4,000-plus caves dot the Ozark highland. In Carter and Shannon counties alone, 287 caves have been identified, with new discoveries adding to that total each year. Just twenty-five years ago fewer than one-tenth that many caverns were known. With such a multiplication, the probability is that many caves remain to be discovered, named, and mapped. And the process of cave making continues, slowly but relentlessly.

Residents of the rivers' hills who have hunted squirrels there for sixty or seventy years insist that springs are fewer now than they were and that those remaining discharge smaller quantities of water than they did. Their memories are of times when every hollow held its own spring where a hot mule and a tired hunter could both find refreshment, but it is hard to imagine a land more blessed with such oases than the hills today.

The water that flows from an Ozark spring has been trapped beneath the surface for days, weeks, or even months and may have traveled many miles before issuing out to the light. It may rise from several hundred feet beneath the water table in a tube, or quietly emerge from several openings into a calm spring pool, or flood up in an unlikely mound of liquid. In any case, it is dolomite, the most common of all sedimentary rocks of the region, that acts as a reservoir for the water. Similar in composition to limestone, dolomite possesses several qualities that make it particularly good stuff for the creation of caves and springs.

Dolostone, as the rock is sometimes called, is porous. It admits water easily, sopping it up and holding it. But in regard to spring development, dolostone's most important property is its solubility. Readily dissolved in even slightly acidic water, dolomite falls easy prey to groundwater that acidifies as it travels through the atmosphere and the surface environment. Precipitation falling in the heavily wooded forests of the Ozarks must pass through a rich layer of decomposing organic matter. On that trip the water picks up carbon dioxide from

The walls and ceiling of Jam-Up Cave exhibit the characteristic breakdown that will eventually spell the cavern's death.

the detritus and is transformed into a highly dilute carbonic acid. To these already favorable conditions for cavern building, add eons of upthrust and fracture in the thick but relatively fragile old dolomite, and the elements for establishing a vast aquifer with a webwork of underground streams are fully in place.

As the water naturally follows the cracks in the rock it enlarges them, eating slowly away. It dissolves the stone into solution and carries it off until a trickle swells into a tube in the rock, and the tube becomes a tunnel, always exposing for itself more and more surface area on which to work.

Erosion within the submerged caverns of today's springs continues in the same way. An interesting twist in the process rests on a quirk of geology. Let in among the dolomite are deposits of chert. When acidic water dissolves the dolomite from around it, the chert, along with varying amounts of insoluble sand and clay, settles to the bottom of the waterway. Lining the floor, this tough flint rock mantle acts as a buffer against further downward erosion. Thus, as raindrops, surface rivulets, and brooks erode their way down into the earth, water of the underground system is instead constantly expanding up and out, wearing away at the walls and roofs of the tunnels through which it runs.

The rate of erosion involved in underground cavern enlargement may also be much greater than we are accustomed to on the earth's surface. Constant flow, heightened acidity such as that caused by acid rain, and contained activity combine to carry huge amounts of dolomite out of the system in solution each year, leaving behind bigger and bigger caverns. As more of the rock's surface is exposed to the slow but tenacious forces at work, the growth rate continues to accelerate. The spring caverns of the Ozarks may be getting bigger, faster than they ever have before.

The source of water supply to the springs is rain soaking into the groundwater network. The piracy and capture of surface streams by such karst features as sinkholes also contributes rainwater to the system. In many places along Ozark creeks and rivers, measurements have shown a suddenly diminished volume of water where a portion of the channel's flow is lost through the streambed to an invisible entrance into the subterranean waterways. Occasionally, the water from such a losing stream can be traced with dyes until it reappears at a spring outlet.

During periods of heavy rain, most springs show an increase in flow, though the change is sometimes more or less than might be expected on the basis of local rainfall. The discrepancies can be attributed to a difference in the amount of precipitation falling at the spring and at the spring's area of supply. Water at Big Spring, for example, has been traced beneath two independent drainages for an underground distance of almost forty miles from where it enters the aquifer to the spring's outlet. A heavy rainfall in that valley forty miles away might even increase the spring's discharge while the sun shines on the spring branch.

Subterranean stream piracy occurs often in the pock-marked hills of the two rivers, but the Current and the Jacks Fork lose little water from their own channels to underground capture. Instead, they are the major beneficiaries of the phenomenon. It is the springs and their sources of supply, including the huge holding tank in rock, that keep especially the Current running full even in times of drought.

The major springs here qualify as deep-circulating, or Artesian, springs, releasing water that has traveled underground and issuing forth at a level substantially above the aquifer. The pressure that forces the flow is supplied by the water table standing above the spring's orifice, resulting in a hydraulic head. The name *Artesian* is derived from the French province of Artois, in which the first well of the sort was bored in 1126 near the city of Calais. That well still flows, uninterrupted.

There are no thermal springs in the Ozarks, all spring water here reflecting instead the approximate mean annual air temperature. In the vicinity of the Current and the Jacks Fork, that puts spring flow at a chilly fifty-six to fifty-nine degrees year-round, with only minor variations. On a hot summer day it is cold enough to cause an ache in even the stoutest of bones. And in zero-degree January, that water—warm by relative measure—steams like hot, clear soup flowing in the branch.

According to their rates of discharge, springs are described as being of the first through the fifth magnitude, with fifth magnitude the smallest and each step representing a tenfold increase in the rate of flow. Because units of measure must change in order to relate to such a wide range of outputs, most of the numbers mean little until the mathematics has been done. But a fifth-magnitude spring releases between 10 and 100 gallons of water per minute, or 14,000 to 140,000 gallons per day. To qualify as a first-magnitude spring, an outlet must let flow more than 45,000 gallons per minute, or at least 65 million gallons in a day's time. Because each of us uses an average of 100 gallons of water per day, even a healthy fifth-magnitude spring pumps enough water in one minute to supply an individual for a day. To take a more concrete example, a monster of the first magnitude such as Big Spring, near Van Buren on the Current River, with its average flow of 276 million gallons every twenty-four hours, churns out enough water to provide a constant supply to more than half the people in the state of Missouri.

Within the boundaries of the Ozark National Scenic Riverways, there lie four springs of the first magnitude, five of the second, and untold others, accounting for the fact that the Current is approximately 70 percent spring water. The only larger river on the continent with as high a percentage of spring water is the Snake River in Idaho, home to even larger outlets. The Jacks Fork shows a lesser, but still substantial, quantity of spring water, especially below the point at which Alley Spring enters its course.

Further classification of these springs can be made by describing whether they flow water from a conduit of rock (tubular), ooze from porous stone or earth (seep, filtration, or sand-boil), or appear along a joint or fault (fracture). There can also be found here ebb-and-flow springs, the rarest of all types. Only about fifty such sources are known to exist, with half the recorded number in the United States and eight in Missouri. Emerald Spring, the source that rises in the back of Little Gem Cave on the Current, is one of only two ebb-and-flow springs in the world known to issue from deep within an air-filled cave. Such springs add to their already substantial mystery the aspect of a measurably fluctuating rate of flow. Each ebb-and-flow spring has a periodicity that can range from one surge per day to as many as eight periods of increased flow in twenty-four hours. And, of course, the springs don't strictly follow even their own rules.

One theory explains the cycling of ebb-and-flow springs by suggesting that their waters at normal (ebb) level pass by an orifice connected to a separate reservoir, or pool. As the primary channel rushes past the opening, a siphon develops and water is drawn from the new source, causing the spring to surge (flow). When the main course of the water fluctuates only slightly or when for some other reason the siphon degrades and finally breaks down, the spring returns to its normal rate of discharge. This sort of behavior is most often noted in systems that are in transition from fully inundated spring conduits to air-filled caves.

That progression from spring to cave is the norm. While speleologists do not agree on all

the details of cave development in the Ozarks, certain basic principles can be outlined. According to current thinking on the subject, almost all the caves in the region were originally formed by dissolution during a time when they were completely submerged. The larger caves were almost certainly part of the subterranean waterway network, serving as conduits in the same way spring caverns do today.

The most widely accepted theory proposes three steps in the manufacture of such solution caves. During the first period, caves were dissolved out of the dolomite. The patterns of the caverns were largely determined by the paths of the fractures and cracks in the rock. Walk in almost any passage in the Ozarks today and down the center of the ceiling there is likely to be a crack. Sometimes unseen or blocked from view, it is most often there nonetheless.

During the ancient period in which this cave carving was occurring beneath the water table, the surface topography was being slowly eroded. From steep hills and hollows of considerable relief, it was worn into a peneplain. As the mountains were reduced, the pressure on the water was lost, the springs flowed with less vigor, and the water in the aquifer came to sit instead of flow. Without a current to sweep away accumulations of sediment and dissolved rock, the underground caverns began to fill. Seeping in from above came fine-grained clay. In some instances, residual chert fragments mixed with this slippery clay to fill the caverns. Evidence of this period of filling can be seen today in caves where remnants of the sticky red ooze cling to the walls from floor to ceiling.

The third step in cave production took place when a series of uplifts again raised the land unevenly. Surface streams were rejuvenated to erode more deeply into the earth's crust, lowering themselves and the water table below the level of the caverns. The small relict springs and streams that remained in the caves were also revitalized and flowed with energy again, washing out all but the remnant masses of clay and chert fill. None of this activity occurred with any precision or rapidity, of course, instead being drawn out over geologic time. Some scientists push the beginnings of Ozark cave development back as far as 100 million years; others believe the caves to be much younger.

With the caverns elevated and air filled, home to small streams and cleared of clay, the decorating of the caves began. The same acidic groundwater that had excavated the passages became responsible for depositing many of the speleothems that adorn most Current and Jacks Fork caves. Whereas before it had dissolved the stone and carried it away in solution, the water now precipitated back out of solution the rock it carried. Dripping and trickling into the still cave air, the water constructed (and continues to add to) stalactites and stalagmites, draperies and columns, soda straws and helictites. Whether the water eats away at rock or leaves it behind depends upon only the tiniest shift in chemistry, and the speed at which the water moves down through the rock strata may have as much to do with that determination as any single factor.

As the formations continue to grow, the caves enter later life. Roofs that were formerly supported by water from beneath begin to break down, dropping huge piles of rubble into the cavern. Clay floors settle, and the weight of accumulating calcite formations tugs at ceiling and walls. Surface erosion wears the cave roof thin. Eventually the strain is too much; the roof collapses into ruin and the cave dies. The region today is well along in

Completely flooding the conduit through which it moves and blocking any view into the spring's workings, the water of Fire Hydrant Spring seems to gush directly from the face of a stone bluff.

another erosion cycle, with the deep springs preparing the next batch of caves and the rivers slowly deepening their channels once again.

While they remain open, the caves of today provide an extraordinary opportunity to move around inside the rock to view geologic processes from the inside out. The closest most of us will ever come to getting a look at a long stretch of spring conduit is in the more easily accessible cave passages where the work the water performed so long ago is still visible.

Cast in a layer of insoluble sandstone on the roofs of several of the region's passageways are the ripples of the shallow seas of prehistory. The "petrified" remains of algae that grew in those seas hundreds of millions of years ago now hang from the cave ceilings. Impurities in the water that built them often color the speleothems brilliantly in shades ranging from the reds of iron oxide to the grays and blacks of manganese oxide. Some Ozark caverns are as heavily decorated with rare formations as caves anywhere. Almost all caves here carry water and retain some colloidal clay fill, making spelunking a messy business. But the sight of fragile and lacelike rimstone dams crafted by the cave streams makes the cleaning up worth the trouble.

Unfortunately, in a few of the more heavily used caves, thoughtless visitors have broken off and stolen decorations left there by eons of dripping, mineral-laden water. Cave environments are fragile. They can be upset easily by the trampling of too many feet or even something as tempting as a simple fire on a rainy afternoon. The smoke from a single campfire can blacken a cavern's ceiling and walls for many years to come.

Human presence in the caves also can disturb animal populations that live there in delicate balance. Bats, the only mammals capable of true flight, rely heavily on the caves in these watersheds as winter hibernation areas and nurseries. One cave near the rivers is occupied by as many as one hundred thousand hibernating Indiana bats from early September until late April each year. The bats in that cave alone represent about one-fifth of the known Indiana bat population. Even a quiet venture into the cave could sufficiently disturb this endangered species of harmless and insect-eating bat to rouse them from their hibernation. Because bats store just enough fat to sustain themselves through the winter and because there are no prevalent insects to replenish that supply during the cold months, a minor disturbance can cost them their lives.

Besides bats, other creatures live either full- or part-time in the caves. Some passages reveal evidence of use by bears, and recent discoveries from not too far away have included the tracks of extinct Pleistocene cats that may have weighed as much as nine hundred pounds. Today, three types of life can be found in the caves, with at least the vast majority of bears and cats long gone from the hills.

Troglobites, such as the rare Ozark cavefish, are subterranean dwellers that have adapted so well to life without light that many lack eyes or pigmentation and could not exist beyond the boundaries of caves or spring caverns. A second group, the troglophiles, do leave caves but could exist completely behind the drip line. The grotto salamander, one of six species of harmless salamanders to be found in Missouri caves, occurs in a larval stage with coloring and sighted eyes. The adults, however, are almost colorless and bear only dark spots where their eyes should be. The larvae can be found in spring branches and spring-fed surface streams, while the adults live only underground. Bats are representative of the third group, trogloxenes, which make use of the caves but must venture out into the sunlit world as well. None of these animals is any threat to man, and all should be left alone when encountered.

The close relationship between caves and springs is further cemented by the appearance

Alley Spring, largest of the Jacks Fork sources, has attracted visitors with its simple beauty for as long as any of the natural wonders of the region.

A heron wades the shoals in search of a meal. (Overleaf)

of many of the same forms of life in the two places. The shared characteristics of a twilight zone and a relatively constant temperature make both caverns and springs home for the limited number of animal species that thrive under these specific conditions, and the moderate climate encourages certain varieties of plants in and around the waters of the springs. Some of the plant species to be found there are indigenous to colder, more northern climes. They were probably carried to the region during the last glacial approach, only to remain in the cool environment of the springs so like their original homes. Watercress (*Nasturtium officinale*) with its pleasantly sharp taste, water milfoils (*Myriophyllum*) growing in large beds, and water starworts (*Callitrichaceae*) are the most common plants of spring branches, where they are joined by the bright green mosses and the slippery algaes.

The rivers' springs and caves are among the region's most popular features, drawing people now as they have since 10,000 B.C. when early early Indians sought them out as campsites and shelters. Later Indian cultures, early settlers, and Civil War bushwhackers all made use of them. Almost every cave along the rivers is thought to have important archaeological significance, and investigations of their secrets are underway. The nineteenth-century mills that drew their operative power from spring flow attracted farmers and their families from miles around. Picnicking at the spring branch was as popular for the Ozarker of a hundred years ago, who refreshed himself there while his grain was ground to meal, as it is for the vacationer of today. The Ozarks' abundant springs have been employed as the focus for resorts, as trout hatcheries, water supplies for the stock farmer, state park sites, sources of domestic water, and even refrigerators to preserve perishables. The springs along the Current and the Jacks Fork have largely escaped use as supplies of municipal water, thanks probably to their isolation and inaccessibility. The spring water is generally of good quality, although officials warn against drinking untested and untreated water. The large quantity of dolomite carried in solution makes the water hard, troublesome in a water heater, but not threatening to human health.

Still, that happy situation is subject to quick and dramatic change. The vast deposits of sedimentary rock through which the springs are recharged are highly porous and quickly accept pollutants of any sort. This aquifer stretches for miles away from the rivers and is mostly unprotected. Agricultural and industrial pollution remain threats to the quality of the water carried in the aquifer, the springs, and the rivers—and therefore to the life they support. The entire water cycle, of which this partnership of springs and rivers is but a small part, was charged with pure water during the melting that ended the last glacial period of the planet's history. As other parts of the world have been forced to learn, that resource is both vital and irreplaceable.

Montauk Springs.   Where the waters of Pigeon Creek are joined by the flow from Montauk Springs in southern Dent County, Missouri, the Current River is born.

Prior to a torrential rainstorm and flood in 1892, Montauk possessed the grandeur befitting a spring at the headwaters of such a river. It was a single outlet spring, rising in a large pool from a depth of two hundred feet or more. But the flood washed in sand and gravel, choking off the source until the flow was divided among several smaller outlets.

Traditionally given as seven, the number of separate spring openings in the valley at Montauk is actually at least twice that many. Five sandboil springs rise in the bottom of

Fishermen in Montauk State Park work the pool above the main lodge.

Montauk Lake, and across Pigeon Creek the valley floor is crowded with pools and seeps. Only one outlet, Bluff Spring, resembles most others along the rivers. An obvious vertical joint creases the small dolomite bluff from which the spring issues. Together, all the outlets in the hollow discharge an average of 53 million gallons of water daily.

The Algonquin Indian name given to the settlement that grew up around the spring is said to have been applied by newcomers homesick for the town they had left in Suffolk County at the eastern tip of Long Island, New York. Montauk is distinguished as the home of the Current River country's first gristmill, built there in 1835 by A. W. Holliman. This mill and three successors turned out meal and flour for the region's farmers until 1925. The mill now standing in Montauk State Park was constructed in 1896.

Beginning with land purchases in 1926, Montauk was preserved as one of Missouri's first state parks. Over the years since, a total of almost twelve hundred acres has been acquired to protect the springs and much of their watershed. The park also includes one of the state's four trout hatcheries, in which carefully monitored spring water is diverted through twenty rearing pools where half a million ten-inch rainbow trout are raised annually for release.

Not far downstream from Montauk lies Tan Vat Hole, where another early mill was situated and where a nineteenth-century tannery operated to process hides into leather. The procedure involved soaking the skins in vats filled with a solution of river water and tannic acid extracted from the bark of the forest's oak trees. The mouth of Inman Hollow, where Tan Vat Hole lies, is the uppermost point at which canoeing is permitted on the river.

Welch Spring and Cave.   Overlooking the rise pool at Welch Spring stand the ruins of a sanitorium built in 1937 by Dr. Christian H. Diehl, who acquired the spring and forty acres of land from the Welch family for a reported price of $800. The sale must have been traumatic for a family so fond of the river that one of their forefathers bore the name Current River Welch.

Dr. Diehl worked to make the spring into a resort and campground, but his dreams proved unprofitable. While staying at the spring to manage his plans, Diehl discovered that the cool, pollen-free air issuing from the cave relieved his hay fever. Assuming that it might do the same for asthma, he had the spring runoff dammed in 1932 until the rising water level blocked off all but one small exit from the cave. The remaining opening he incorporated into the back wall of the sanitorium. By 1937, Diehl's hospital was ready for operation, and patients were being sought to take the innovative cure. Unfortunately, Dr. Diehl died in 1940 without having proved his theory concerning the remedial powers of the airs of Welch Spring Cave.

With the construction of Dr. Diehl's dam, the flow from Welch Spring was split, with some of the water spilling directly from the pool over slippery rocks to the river six feet below. The remainder travels a branch parallel to the river for a quarter mile until the flows join. The old dam can still be seen just below the water's surface, running obliquely across the calm rise pool. The longer runoff was the later site of a trout farm and fisherman's resort that fared no better than Dr. Diehl's innovative designs.

The spring issues from beneath a bluff just 50 feet off the river. Below the water level in the dolomite is the main entrance to Welch Cave. Closed to visitors, the cave holds a

The sanitorium at Welch Spring was built of native rock by local stonemasons paid fifty cents per day for their labors in 1937. Dr. Christian H. Diehl, the project's architect, believed that vapors rising from the spring cavern would cure his patients of their asthma.

A narrow riffle on the Jacks Fork reflects the wild nature of the upper river.

pool 150 feet long by 75 feet wide, with water rising to within a few feet of the ceiling. The cave is heavily decorated and comprises several large rooms in its 2,000 feet of passageway. Welch Spring discharges 78 million gallons of water per day, making it the eighth largest spring in the state and adding greatly to the size of the upper Current River at the junction of spring branch and stream.

Cave Spring. Caught in an early stage of transition between one part of the subterranean system and the other, the Cave Spring complex is both cave and spring. Delivering an average of 21 million gallons of water per day at river level, the system can be entered by boat for a distance of about 100 feet. Beyond that there is simply no more cave. But beneath the boater in the back of the cave is an almost perfectly vertical rock tube 30 feet in diameter and 155 feet deep. This shaft is joined at its base by horizontal conduits that supply it with water. Divers have explored both the vertical tube and the horizontal supply lines and have found evidence of the continuing dissolution of the dolomite, protruding masses of chert, and sand on the bottom of the tunnels.

Open to the river and maintaining a year-round temperature of fifty-eight degrees, Cave Spring makes a snug home for fish during winter when the stream water becomes uncomfortably cold. Because it harbors fish in this manner, the spot is also known as Fishing Spring Cave.

A few hundred feet downstream from Cave Spring in the bankside bluff is the entrance to Wallace Well, a small cave that extends back into the hillside. A hole in the floor of Wallace Well grants a rare look inside a spring as it opens to a subterranean lake 20 feet below the floor of the cave. Connected by a conduit to Cave Spring, the water in Wallace Well lake is also linked to water in a sinkhole almost a mile away. Called Devil's Well, the sinkhole appears from the surface to close off at a depth of about 40 feet but actually opens again to reveal a lower room that houses a lake 400 feet long by 100 feet wide, with water depths of up to 200 feet. Such dimensions place this hidden reservoir among the largest cave lakes in the nation. Four waterfalls and an unknown number of springs feed the huge pool, helping to supply its 22-million gallon storehouse.

Both Wallace Well and Devil's Well are part of the Cave Spring complex, storing water in remote pockets. Divers have made the underwater journey from Cave Spring to the lake in Wallace Well, and dyes introduced at Devil's Well have appeared at Cave Spring in a week's time.

Pulltite Spring. Not far downstream from Cave Spring lies Pulltite, one of the Current's liveliest and most refreshing springs. There, along a branch lined with redbud, watercress, and wildflowers, the water churns its way out of a gentle hollow past a log cabin built in one of the traditional architectural styles of the Ozarks.

The one-and-one-half-story cabin was built in 1913 by a group of St. Louis businessmen and is made of logs arranged vertically in the French tradition rather than the more common horizontal orientation. The lodge, with its huge stone fireplace, is the last of several structures to stand along the Pulltite branch. Three mills relied on Pulltite's flow for power over the years, and temporary shelters housed lumbermen there during the heydey of the logging industry. Pilings still visible in the river mark the spot not far downriver at which a railroad connecting the lumber camps with the mill crossed the water, circa 1910 to 1920.

Missouri's sixth largest spring, Blue Spring on the Current nestles in a deep hollow where mink occasionally can be seen at play around the water.

The Pulltite name was born in an era when families bringing their grain to the mill encountered a steep hill on the final approach to the river. Coming down that hill with a full load required skidding the wagon wheels. But it was the drive back out of the hollow, the rig laden with sacks of meal, that caused the mules to pull their harness tight—thus *Pulltite*. The old wagon road traveled by those settlers is no longer visible, having gone unused for decades. Vestiges of the same era's Cedargrove–to–Round Spring road can be seen in the Pulltite campground on the opposite side of the river, however.

The flow at Pulltite fluctuates more than that of many springs, having ranged over the years between a high of 92 million gallons per day and as little as 4 million gallons. Pulltite also suffers more than many springs during times of drought.

Just downstream from the branch, in the streamside rock, issues Fire Hydrant Spring, or as it is also known, Barrel Spring. This little gusher pours into the river from a small cave and releases almost 3 million gallons of water daily, with fluctuations in flow not necessarily tied to those of the nearby bigger spring.

Overland, due west of Pulltite, lies the Sunklands, an area rich in karst features including caves, sinkholes, and marshy lakes. Upstream from the spring is Rockhouse Cave, and just downstream one of many unnamed springs offers its small flow to the river at water level.

Round Spring and Round Spring Caverns.   Uncounted years ago, the roof over the rise pool at Round Spring collapsed. What had been a part of the subterranean supply system became instead the spring pool itself. That collapse may have been the result of a natural breakdown of the former cave's ceiling. It also might have occurred after a new, lower spring outlet developed, thus dropping the water level in the cavern until all support for the roof's arch was gone. Or perhaps, as lore would have it, an Osage Indian brave became so angered by insults from his companions that he struck the ground with his war club, using such force that the tremors he produced caused the cave-in.

In any event, a jumble of boulders from the collapse now closes off the supply conduit to the spring at a depth of fifty-four feet. The circular rise pool exposed in the collapse delivers its water to the branch from beneath a portion of the roof that remained intact and now forms a natural bridge. Approximately 26 million gallons per day flow deceptively from the lazy-looking spring down a sparkling branch of considerable length. The water supply to the spring is thought to come in part from Spring Valley, just to the southwest.

Up that valley only a short walk, in the Eminence Dolomite formation, sits Round Spring Caverns. Among the largest caves nearby, it consists of nearly a mile of heavily decorated passageways. Most of the cave's speleothems remain in excellent condition. The cavern was discovered in 1931 by two men from Cuba, Missouri, who were looking specifically for a cave to develop into a commercial enterprise near the newly formed Round Spring State Park. In an area as rich in history and archaeological wealth as this, the cave almost certainly was known by earlier peoples, too.

The cavern consists of two wings, the left slightly longer than the right. These main branches intersect at a side passage that forms the entrance. A trip through the cave offers the visitor a chance to see an unusually wide variety of cave decoration, the bones of bear and opossum, and many evidences of the ancient forces that combined to create the caverns.

Eighteen miles downstream from Round Spring is Two Rivers, where the Jacks Fork and the Current join.

Blue Spring and Jam-Up Cave. Ten cave-filled miles from where the North Prong and the South Prong meet to form the Jacks Fork River is located one of two Blue Springs on these streams. Situated opposite one of the most picturesque gravel bars on the upper Jacks Fork, this spring flows about 3 million gallons a day from a dolomite bluff and around boulders that split the runoff into three courses. At times of high discharge, the water quickly turns cloudy, reflecting the theory that much of this spring's supply is drawn from agricultural lands to the north.

A concrete dam built across the mouth of the small pool shows the date 1937. At normal water levels, the spring discharges through a break in the dam and at higher water completely covers it. Within a few hundred feet of the spring are six caves, bearing the names Blue Slot, Blue Cleft, Blue Aerie, Blue Spring, Blue Lower, and Flue. These caves open at various elevations above the river and must have been outlets for the spring flow at earlier times.

The three miles of river immediately downstream from Blue Spring to Jam-Up Cave hold many small springs and caves. During periods of high water, creeks can be heard reverberating from where they fall, unseen, into the backs of the many caverns. Jam-Up Cave itself is home to two such cascades.

One of the largest and most famous cave entrances in the state, the main arch opening to Jam-Up Cave, where columbine and jack-in-the-pulpit grow plentifully, is only one of several ways into the cavern. This huge entry funnels directly into a large room stretching 350 feet back to a lake where waterfalls pour past a spherical boulder wedged in a great crack. The floor of the room is littered with breakdown from the ceiling, some of it in pieces the size of a small house. It is as if the cave were the arena for a game played by messy giants. A small spring in the wall of the cave one-fourth of the way in adds to the flow of the creek, and in wet weather a rain of constant drips falls from the ceiling to splash on the rocks below.

The stream that drains the cave lake and tumbles to the river well below, Jam-Up Creek, is a surface stream completely captured by a large sinkhole in the valley above the cave. Disappearing into the swallowhole, the stream reappears when it cascades into the back of the cavern. This creek, which drains nineteen square miles of country and hauls debris into the cave during floods, is a textbook example of how subterranean stream piracy works.

Rymer Spring. Rymer Spring is an unexpected surprise to the boater on the Jacks Fork who encounters it in the unlikely setting of a bluffless flat. This gem is a detailed miniature of some of the rivers' more famous sources, but with a distinct character and appeal of its own.

A rise pool two feet deep and five feet above river level releases water over a slide of mossy rocks. A bridge of stone and earth extends from the heavily striated dolomite wall behind the spring to a central island, giving the impression of a horseshoe shape. The hazy blue color common to spring water is accentuated at Rymer, and the fifty-six degree temperature is colder than most.

Rymer is an ebb-and-flow spring, sometimes showing six or seven periods of significantly increased flow per day. At other times, the rate of discharge is surprisingly constant. Apparently, both above and below certain discharge levels, the rate does not change markedly. But in some middle range, perhaps when a natural siphon is operating, the surges associated with such springs occur. It is difficult to report a rate of flow for Rymer, but it probably averages about three hundred thousand gallons per day.

A quiet backwater on a downstream section of the Current is home to the still water and heavy cover preferred by largemouth bass.

Alley Spring. Alley Spring is the largest of the Jacks Fork springs and the seventh largest in the state, pumping 81 million gallons daily. Surging from beneath a hundred-foot high dolomite bluff, its water mounds slightly in a one-acre pool before cresting a rock dam and splashing its way down a half-mile branch. The rise pool reaches a depth of thirty-two feet before necking down to a steeply sloping supply tunnel.

The 170-foot-long dam on the mill pond is composed of river boulders and cement. It channels a portion of the vigorous spring flow through a headrace that drives a turbine wheel at the Alley Spring Roller Mill. The mill building as it stands today was completed in 1895, with four of the original milling machines from what was one of the most up-to-date mills in the Ozarks still in place.

The first water-powered mill at Alley dates to 1869 and the partnership of William Barksdale and John Dougherty. Enlarged, damaged by flood, and rebuilt as it stands, the mill was once the center of a community that included a post office, a general store, a blacksmith shop, a sawmill, and a school. At its peak, the mill's machinery could grind fifty barrels of flour a day. It proved to be such a popular place that there was a time when patrons had to wait in line to have their grain processed. The spring branch was the natural resting spot for the unhurried Ozarker waiting his turn, and it was there that the tradition of a vacation at Alley Spring began.

The spring is named for John Alley, an early settler and one of the region's prominent farmers. Although history records no direct connection between Alley and the spring or the mill, it may be that he worked to help construct the earliest buildings there.

By 1924, industrialization had made it possible for even the isolated Ozark farmer to purchase flour from the store more cheaply than he could have his own grain milled, and the operation at Alley Spring fell into obsolescence. At about the same time, paved roads were bringing ever larger numbers of people to the region's points of interest, and the State of Missouri purchased the spring, mill building, and 427 acres of land to create the fourth of her state parks.

Legend records that at one time the spring's flow suddenly stopped and the level in the pool dropped five feet. After a twelve-hour lull, the flow resumed, but what before had been clean and pure water was brown and muddy. Alley Spring water remained cloudy for days to come, according to the tale. No date for the event is recorded, but it is possible that the interruption coincided with the collapse of a sinkhole nearby. A portion of the water appearing at Alley Spring has been traced eleven miles from a large sinkhole near the town of Summersville to the northwest.

Fourteen miles downriver from the spring branch, the Jacks Fork meets the Current at the Two Rivers junction.

Blue Spring. Missouri is home to nine Blue Springs, two Blue Hole Springs, two Blue Grass Springs, a Blue Lick, and a Blue Stem Spring. But the Blue Spring on the Current River sets the standard for them all and for blue water everywhere. Called the "Spring of the Summer Sky" by the Osage Indians, no running water anywhere is a match for the cold, hard blue seen here.

Explanations for the depth of the shade include the theory that mineral particles carried in the water scatter the reflection of light in a way that enhances the blue. Others say the

On Rocky Creek, a tributary of the Current River, the unremitting rush of water has polished even the hardest of igneous rocks to a slippery sheen.

Beneath a sky of scudding clouds, Big Spring's flow swirls into the Current River.

depth of the spring influences the color. That could be the case; at 256 feet, Blue Spring is the deepest in Missouri and deeper than many drilled wells.

Mink and other wildlife are especially drawn to this spring's pool, where almost 90 million gallons of water rise each day to surge down one of the wildest branches in the Ozarks. A portion of the flow, which makes the outlet Missouri's sixth largest, is pirated from Logan Creek. A tributary of the Black River, Logan Creek lies in a separate watershed entirely and eventually gives up all its water to underground capture.

The site of an early trading post on the river, Blue Spring is steeped in hill legend. One story that persists around the spring tells of a turn-of-the-century timberman who was working the steep country above the Blue Spring bluff when only the depth of the spring averted a tragedy. This woodsman, alone except for his blind mule, had trained the animal to skid logs from the cutting site to a ridge road where, with a certain shake of his traces, he released his load and returned to the woodcutter for the next. This smart mule lost his way in the dense woods on one trip and plunged off the bluff into the spring with a considerable splash. Hearing the commotion, the timberman ran to find his mule unharmed and taking advantage of his situation by enjoying a refreshing swim. In the style of the Ozarks, the woodcutter laid down his ax and joined the animal in a break from work.

Just a mile upstream from Blue Spring is the sweep in the river known as Owl's Bend, where several hundred acres of rich bottomland were home to Indian encampments and, later, one of the most prosperous early farms. Also nearby is Powder Mill Creek with its several springs for supply and the river crossing where one of the last water-powered ferries in the state ran.

Gravel Spring. Little-known Gravel Spring, rising on the east side of the river downstream from multicolored Paint Rock Bluff, has escaped exploitation and development. There is no record of settlement here, where almost 11 million gallons per day are added to the already substantial volume of the Current River.

Minus a spring branch and without a bluff of its own, Gravel Spring sneaks into the flow from a small and unspectacular gravel bar. Behind the mound of chert is a sort of spring pool open to the river that tempts the boater to test his nerve in the fifty-eight degree water. The river is wide and easy here, and the spring water appears exceptionally clear and sparkling as it ripples across the tan shoal.

Deer can often be seen crossing the river in the vicinity of Gravel Spring during those seasons when the lower river's relatively heavy motorboat travel is at a minimum.

Big Spring. High on the list of the world's largest single outlet springs, Big Spring lets loose huge tides of water each day. Amounts have ranged all the way up to an estimated 840 million gallons on a June day in 1928, enough water to meet the needs of every Missourian, with plenty left to fill every bathtub in the state.

The stream created by Big Spring is deep and wide, more a small river than a spring branch. It is big enough that johnboats powered by large outboards cruise well up into it to load tourists interested in a powerboat ride on the Current.

Water appears to come from everywhere at Big Spring, and in fact there are several openings, but the main outlet boils up in an unrestrained mound that captivates the onlooker with its size and force. This flood courses out of an underwater cave with a collapsed roof and around the boulders in its path. Attempting to explore the supply lines to the massive

spring, divers have been thwarted by the sheer pressure of the water pushing them back. A glimpse of the system is available from a hole in the nearby rockfall, and huge caverns must lie beyond the mouth. It has been calculated that the network feeding Big Spring dissolves and removes 175 tons of dolomite each day.

Big Spring water has been traced from near the town of Mountain View and the watershed of the Eleven Point River. Despite lingering stories that this spring's water travels from Montana, Lake Michigan, or other faraway places, there is no evidence to support anything but a regional source for the torrent that streams from the ground at Big Spring.

Established as one of the early state parks, with more than five thousand acres, there was little development at the site until 1933 when the Civilian Conservation Corps undertook the construction of trails and bridges and the building of dikes to contain the branch channel. Many of the buildings standing there today are of the same vintage.

Big Spring marks the downstream point at which the nature of the Current River has undergone its inevitable change. From an early gradient of almost nine feet of drop per mile of travel, the pace by now has slowed to a drop of less than three feet in a mile. The river has become lazy. Canoeing is enjoyable largely only to here, and powerboats become more numerous in the vicinity of Van Buren. The broad, deep, and slow waters of the lower river continue their course past the town of Doniphan and across the Arkansas line until giving up even their name at the confluence with the Black River.

At a canoe camp established on the gravel above Round Spring, late winter's high water has left leaf litter in the willow branches.

4.

Devastation

THE Current and Jacks Fork countryside is convoluted and secretive, full of hiding places where man's relatively brief history on the land easily gets tucked away and lost. Quick-growing vegetation claims any space left to it, and the forest swallows up the metal, stone, and wooden remnants of occupation. The human stories surrounding any deserted place are soon left completely to short-lived and fault-prone memory. Only the most cataclysmic event leaves on the land any enduring trace.

If you stand on a gravel bar in early morning, while slabs of mist lift into the perfect air, the setting will seem ages-old, with the look and feel of an untouched wilderness. There is only the overabundance of flint gravel to recall that time when the hills were laid bare and erosion swept the soil and stone from the slopes. Walking among the many varieties of forest trees and the bright, blooming wildflowers, you'll find it hard to imagine that man has ever changed anything here. Only the dense underbrush and closely spaced trunks suggest that this second- and third-growth forest is a new and externally influenced succession. The rivers themselves appear to flow out of history undisturbed except in those places where pilings still poke from the surface to crease the current, relics of the logging days when heavy bridges spanned the water.

These clues alone, along with a maze of vestigial logging roads, mark the face of the land to point back to that time when the whine of the mill saws displaced peacefulness in the woods, when steam locomotives chugged out of the mountains loaded down with huge logs, when the tall timber was ripped from the hills and sacrificed to a nation consumed by development and westward expansion. Those old-timers who can remember the big pine forests grow fewer each year. They are heard from less often and listened to less carefully as the generations recede and newcomers assume that their own visions of the land have always prevailed.

Botanists have been unable to agree completely about the size and composition of the primordial forest and the extent to which open prairie was mixed with woodland. And only in a rare, isolated sanctuary is any of the virgin timber still harbored. There, surviving trees tower over surrounding upstarts. The most accessible such place is a stand of shortleaf pine cleaved by Missouri Highway 19 on its trip south from Round Spring to the town of Eminence. Standing in that small patch of venerable evergreens, the imagination strains to put back in place all the old trees; to recreate the long, unbroken view between enormous trunks; to replace the open understory and grass-covered forest floor so that conditions, at least in the mind's eye, will be as they were.

The deep and secluded woods of places like Stillhouse Hollow afforded hideouts for Civil War bushwhackers and prohibition-era moonshiners alike.

Where maples cluster, autumn is bright with yellow and orange.

Ancient igneous rock flows appear only rarely among sedimentary dolomite, but underlay the more recent deposits everywhere in the region.

Those virgin woodlands had been home to human beings for perhaps 12,000 years and remained largely uninfluenced by the presence of man among them when the saws finally brought them down. Big-game hunters clad in skins and bearing rock-tipped spears first stalked mastodon, tapir, and giant beaver among the mix of spruce and deciduous trees that flourished in the wetter climate of 10,000 B.C. When later prehistoric Indian cultures visited the Current and the Jacks Fork, they adapted to the geography, taking advantage of the many caves and overhanging bluffs for shelter. The particular lay of the land influenced their social and cultural development, foretelling similar relationships between the rivers' hills and almost every subsequent population. Today, the stories of those prehistoric residents are being reconstructed at a number of archaeological investigations along the riverbanks. Early discoveries suggest that the region may rank among the nation's most important to the study of archaic cultures.

The area's historic Indians lived on the open prairie to the west and claimed the forests as hunting territory. Returning each year to hunt the plentiful game and to collect valuable flint from which to craft arrowheads and tools, the Osage tribes developed an attachment to the land that persisted even after they had officially relinquished all claims to the territory in an 1825 treaty. Warlike bands continued to hunt and raid near the rivers, doing much as they pleased, until almost 1860.

It was the imposing Osage whom the French trappers in the Ozarks first encountered sometime around the year 1700. Moving south down the Mississippi, the French came in quest of the silver and gold they believed the mountains to hold. They found no metal more precious than lead but trapped for their prized furs peaceably among the Osage, developing complex trade relations with the Indians. By 1725 the friendship between the two populations had grown so close that a group of Indians was escorted to France where its members became the talk of Paris. Unfortunately, the ways of the Missouri woods suited the French no better than high society appealed to their Osage friends; the Frenchmen managed few settlements and little success off the land.

Early Spanish efforts in the Ozarks fared even more poorly, hindered as they were by hate-filled contact with the native Osage. Not long after acquiring official control of the territory in 1762, the Spanish government invited the more friendly and "civilized" Shawnee and Delaware tribes to occupy lands in the interior, including sites along the Current and Jacks Fork rivers. There, they were expected to act as a buffer between the worried Spanish and the bellicose Osage. The Shawnee population of that day left as large a legacy as any of the early people, contributing place names still in use without altering the appearance of the resilient land.

When in 1803, the Louisiana Purchase doubled the size of the United States, foreign dominion ended and the way was opened for American settlement. The first majestic forest was still safely in place when farmsteaders and hunters arrived during the early decades of the nineteenth century. By 1800, most of Missouri had been settled, but the Courtois Hills in the rugged interior remained isolated and undeveloped. Topography played a large part in life on the Ozark land, as much of the modernizing traffic to the frontier continued to skirt the borders of the steep terrain, seeking more convenient routes west across flat land or along big water.

An early morning mist closes the Pulltite Spring branch in a cloak of fluid mystery.

Overland by wagon from Kentucky, Tennessee, and Virginia came the settlers who would finally claim the territory. Accustomed to a life in hills very much like the Ozarks, they were possessed of a Scotch-Irish pride instilled in them by their stout forebears. The early Americans who first laid down the traditional Ozark ways held close to their staunch Presbyterianism and to the skills and wiles required by a self-sufficient life in unsullied country. Some had opened ground for farming before, when they moved from coastal settlements into the mountains just to the west.

The countryside to which they came encouraged a simple life of solitude and independence. Isolating hollows and rivers too deep and swift for simple crossing made travel difficult. In their new lives most of the settlers realized not great wealth but the bounty that the land freely offered. Success did not demand the same domineering attitude required of frontiersmen who settled more western wildernesses. Pioneers here homesteaded first in the rich agricultural river bottoms. Later arrivals and those with more nomadic values settled upslope and relied largely upon hunting and stock raising for their livelihoods.

It was a land full of options for the exercise of personal preference. Rough and demanding to be sure, it nonetheless supported cattle, horses, mules, and the many hogs that produced the most favored meat. Corn and other vegetables were easily raised in the cooperative climate, and fruit, nuts, and honey for sweetener were plentiful in the wild. For those nonfarmers in the population the hunting of wild turkey, white-tailed deer, and smaller game meant easy subsistence. Few pastures were cleared by even the most devoted agriculturalists; the forage in the woods, glades, and river bottoms provided amply for stock that was simply turned out onto the open range.

Timber was cut to fashion cabins, the most luxurious of which took the distinctive Ozark style of a steeply peaked roof to allow room for a sleeping loft among the rafters, a dog trot between separate buildings, large porches front and rear to cool the hot summer breezes, and a huge stone hearth that served as the center of family life. Towns were slow to develop, harboring only a fraction of the self-reliant settlers during the early 1800s.

Where few before them had done more than pass by, families like the Chiltons and the Carters made their stands. The bottomland not far downstream from Van Buren was home to both clans' first farms before 1820. From Virginia with Benjamin Carter came his young son Zimri, who would grow to become one of the rivers' most successful farmers. Not long after arriving in Missouri, a Carter neighbor by the name of Thomas Boggs Chilton sent word back home that life on the Current River was superior, and cousin Thomas Coot Chilton emigrated too. It is for old T. C. that Coot Chute, just downstream from the junction of the two rivers, is so lyrically named. By 1840 there were twenty-four separate Chilton farms thriving along the banks. Big families and a love of the country that goes well beyond mere ownership hold the descendants of the first settlers near the streams today, their lives still imbued with the spirit of the old ways and customs.

Even so momentous an event as the Civil War left little mark upon the land, with the nature of the fighting dictated largely by the terrain. No physical scars remain to recall the devastation and terror of the times; no forts were ever constructed; no battle sites have been preserved. Even that cannon said to have been abandoned by Union troops, retreating from an encampment overlooking Watercress Spring after suffering through the bitterly cold winter of 1862–1863, now is said to rest deep in the choked-off spring pool, covered by silt and chert.

Ranks of Eastern red cedar march across an abandoned field, providing a winter backdrop for stark saplings.

If the countryside was little affected by the fighting, the same cannot be said of the small population. Deep hollows afforded safe hideouts for bushwhackers, murderers, and cut-throats for whom the war became an excuse for violence. They fought according to their own rules, or no rules at all. Deep in the hills, the period from 1855 to 1875 was one of revolt and strife. Criminal attack and bloody revenge for real or imagined transgressions between formerly friendly neighbors disrupted peaceful lives.

Few around the rivers held slaves or even personal reasons for an opinion on war issues. But those who were believed to be in support of the other side, no matter which side that was, often had their farmhouses burned, their crops destroyed, and their livestock summarily slaughtered. Many of the guerrillas worked as much for personal gain as for allegiance to a cause, and their marauding killed or drove away even the most committed settlers. Population growth effectively ceased; Shannon County, for example, grew by only forty-seven people during the 1860s as the countryside reverted to an unpopulated forest. In the people, there has evolved from those days of distress and from their Scotch-Irish heritage a certain wariness of strangers, a cautious reserve that is so traditionally mixed with an equally inherent hospitality as to have become a distinct part of the Ozark personality.

But the land remained constant and reliable even while disruptive events raged, strengthening the people's tie to the ground and to their developing society. A well-rooted faith and regular churchgoing provided a solid core for many lives, as well as a focus for social activity. Beyond church, life centered on the home place. The isolating effect of the topography worked to keep change out, creating a gap filled by steadfast reliance on proven ways of making do. Fads and waves of influence that moved through the culture generally reached the rivers late and thinned down. Looking to themselves for their answers, Ozarkers opted for customs over laws, family ties over social connections, and individuality over any group identity. Like those cedar fenceposts that border his farm, the Ozarker relies on the ground for his anchor and his security.

*   *   *

The legacy of adapting to the land and not battling it, of harvesting the offered wealth and asking little more, of being economically and socially self-sustaining had begun in the native populations and endured the Civil War as well as its resultant turmoil. It outlasted the influx of a diverse new population after the war. The old ways and the old woods survived together in good health right up until that day in 1871 when two men got off the train at the end of the line in Ironton, Missouri, and rode toward the timbered hills of the rivers.

O. II. P. Williams and his son-in-law E. B. Grandin were on a scouting expedition. New England forests had been cut over and the pair recognized that pressure on the Great Lakes' pineries promised soon to deplete them. New wood was required by reconstruction and the growth of a bustling nation. The yellow pines that had stood for so long exactly filled the bill. Williams and Grandin recognized their opportunity and purchased 30,000 acres during their trip, at an average price of one dollar per acre. Those lands, added to later at even lower prices, became the basis for the Missouri Lumber and Mining Company.

A bed of wildflowers softens the forest floor in the Pulltite campground.

Roots and rocks struggle to maintain their places against the force of Big Spring's immense tides.

Spiny hawthorn branches and poison ivy decked out in autumn raiment form a menacing web around the small blossoms of the white heath aster at the side of the Ozark Trail.

That firm was one of three giants that eventually cut almost 1.5 billion board feet of lumber from 375,000 acres of hillslope. The effects on both the countryside and the people would prove to be catastrophic; a way had been found to change the woods.

The two owners quickly hired well-known Pennsylvania lumberman John Barber White to head their Missouri operations, and by 1880 his first mill was slicing pine trees to boards under steam-generated power. Three years later, a spur of the Iron Mountain Railroad on which Williams and Grandin had first ridden into the country was completed to the Current River town of Doniphan; it became possible for lumber transported downstream to be shipped from the railhead there.

But the terrain made moving the mill's output inconvenient and expensive. When the railroad refused to come to White's Mill for the product, the four-year-old operation had to be shut down, and nearly 125 local men employed there experienced their first layoff, a portent of economic events to come.

In 1850, 94 percent of the residents of the counties flanking the rivers were engaged primarily in farming. By 1880, the booming population was much more diverse. Following the logging industry into the region came specialists to oversee the railroads, the big saws, the steam power plants, and the construction of what became the world's largest sawmill of the day. Many farmers were lured from their subsistence existences by the coming of the cash economy and the prospect of work for pay.

When a deal was finally signed with the Kansas City, Fort Scott, and Memphis Railroad to haul sawed lumber, J. B. White had the mill reestablished at the company town of Grandin. Built solely for the purpose of accommodating the loggers and their labors, Grandin was complete by 1888, and the sawing began again. When the railroad spur reached the mill from the west in 1889, 6 million board feet of lumber had been cut, dried, and stacked and was waiting to be loaded onto the Current River Railroad's flatcars for the west. Having been disappointed once by the larger rail lines serving the east, White concentrated all future dealings on markets in the opposite direction. Soon after the first shipment left the mill yard, J. B. White moved to Kansas City to oversee the marketing of his company's products.

Known throughout the industry as a conservationist, White espoused the philosophy of replanting where forests had been cut and believed in leaving behind enough rootstock to prevent erosion. He anticipated the depletion of the finest lumber and called for the use of poorer grades wherever they would serve. But he was foremost a businessman under pressure from his corporate superiors to produce a profit in what quickly became a highly competitive industry in the Ozarks. White gave his bosses what they wanted; none of the profits went for reforestation.

The company town of Grandin grew large, housing a population of 3,000 by 1900, all lumber company employees. A total of fifty miles of tramline was laid into the dense forest and as many as seven steam engines pulled railcars full of timber to the mill. To keep the huge operation working, land had to be snapped up, and deeds became confused or ignored. Competition between companies forced races to get to the timber, clear-cut it, and get out whole sections of forest. Between 100,000 and 200,000 board feet were sawed out at Grandin each day; yearly capacity totaled 70 million board feet of lumber. By the end of 1902, in just fourteen-years' time, the Missouri Lumber and Mining Company alone had cut 648 million board feet, working six days a week, twenty hours a day. Supplying the

The calm waters of a Jacks Fork pool reflect a perfect image of the fall's brightening foliage.

The mountains give way to fertile bottomland on a Current River farm.

spinning saws with fodder required the trees from sixty acres of Ozark countryside every single day.

Workers lived in company-owned shotgun houses, so-called because a blast fired at the front door would have hit everyone within the narrow and well-aligned rooms. Unskilled laborers earned $1.50 per day and paid $3 per month in rent for a three-room house. Company stores, well stocked with factory-made shirts (25 cents), overalls (50 cents with full bib, 35 cents without), and more exotic goods of every description, supplied needs and newly discovered desires. Credit was available to those still honing their skills with the new concept of cash, and much of what was paid out in wages returned to the stores when employees became fascinated with the exchange of dollars for goods and services. Many workers abandoned their gardens altogether and bought all their food from the grocery's shelves. The tradition of bartering for those few essentials that could not be made or grown soon gave way to the convenience of purchasing every need. Self-reliance was chased from the hills by the promise of a life of ease and the dawning of more complicated social, political, and economic systems.

Life in Grandin and later in West Eminence was strictly ordered, with little of the rowdyism usually associated with such towns allowed. Single workers resided in boardinghouses segregated according to sex, and repeated fighting or a single instance of drunkenness was cause for dismissal. There were no saloons in town, but a surprising array of conveniences was available, including a barber shop, a well-equipped fire department, and an iron shop where all the tools of the logging trade were manufactured. Medical care came at a bargain price from the company doctor; churches, schools, and the hospital all stood on company turf. Electricity came to the mill towns before it reached many more "advanced" regions because of the availability of power from the mills' boilers.

Life in town must have been engagingly convenient and more comfortable than that back on the farm, but the work was hard. Sawyers and support crews left town on trains or paddle-wheeled boats called gas boats for sites where timber was being cut. There, for periods of up to ninety days, they camped in tents, slept on straw beds, and cut wood with crosscut saws at all seasons of the year. Those virgin pines on which they concentrated their early efforts stood eighty to ninety feet tall and grew to five feet in diameter. When the string-straight trunks came crashing down, they were limbed, cut to sixteen- or eighteen-foot lengths, skidded by mule to the nearest logging road, loaded onto wagons pulled by more mules, and finally transferred to flatcars on one of the tramlines in the woods. Connecting the lumber camps with the mills, the tram railroads ran the mountain ridges on narrow-gauge track laid by specialized crews. When all the timberland served by a tramline had been sawed out, the track was taken up and moved to a new cutting site.

Biggest of all the backwoods camps that ringed the mill town of West Eminence during the later days of the logging industry's occupation was Camp 12. Home to timbermen served by their own doctor, grocery store, semipermanent housing, and stable facilities for the eighty head of mules that worked the forests with the men, Camp 12 left no mark that is visible seventy years later.

In addition to being railroaded from the forests, trees were skidded to the riverbanks, accumulated there, then set loose in downstream log drives. Eight to ten men usually accompanied a drive, which took as long as a week or more on the water. Using flat-bottomed boats to keep track of the timber, the men tended to freeing the jams that occurred frequently on the twisting trip downriver. Logs inclined to sink had to be rescued and spiked to more buoyant wood to keep them from being lost. The irresistible force of the running water, logs weighing several tons, headstrong mules inclined to bolt, and steam trains on steep grades combined to make the timbermen's jobs difficult and often dangerous, with injuries commonplace.

The great logs bobbed down both rivers from origination points that by the turn of the century lined the banks. They floated to a spot, not far from Van Buren, where a boom across the flow halted their travel. Known as the Chinese Wall, the boom was built of a raft of fourteen-inch pine beams strung from bank to bank. An endless chain conveyor hauled logs from the river for transportation to the mill at Grandin or elsewhere. The railhead was situated across the stream from the town of Van Buren and bore the name of Chicopee.

Modern choice of craft can be traced back to those years of toil on the rivers. It is unlikely that an Ozarker today will be found on the water in anything but a traditional johnboat. Long, less than a yard wide at the waterline, and traditionally made of wood, the flat-bottomed boats draw only a few inches of water over a shoal. They are especially utilitarian for fishing and gigging, today's river business. An unstable canoe of some modern wonder material is, in the book of most, an unfit craft for humans. After all, shift a healthy wad of chewing tobacco from one jowl to the other, and the whole outfit is liable to tip over.

As the storehouse of ancient pine was decimated at the turn of the century, markets were discovered for the remaining hardwoods. Lumber companies diversified into oak when continuing railroad expansion created a need for crossties. In some instances as many as three thousand ties were laid for every mile of track set down, producing a huge demand. By 1896 Henry H. Smalley had partnered with an existing firm to found the H. H. Smalley Tie and Timber Company, first of many crosstie suppliers to work the hills.

Most of the ties fashioned from oak that grew around the Current and the Jacks Fork were cut to shape, or hacked, in the forest. At stumpside, men expert with broadax hewed the tough wood to six-by-eight or seven-by-nine inches before the downstream trip began. The railroads preferred hand-hewn ties to sawed timbers and paid a premium for the handmade product. As they had for the logging industry, many of the workers for the tie companies came off local farms, drawn to the work by the cash they could make. Farmsteaders relinquished their lands to build rough shacks in the forests near stands of virgin oak, living there until the wealth played out before moving on in search of more good trees. Some worked independently, while others contracted their labor to Smalley or his competitors. Pay for a single hand-hewn railroad tie in 1900 averaged twenty-five cents, delivered at the railhead at Chicopee, and a good tie-hack could cut ten to twelve eight-foot lengths in a day's work.

For a time, ties were floated downriver loose in drives, much as the larger logs had been moved. But as the logging concerns attracted ever bigger populations and commerce expanded, farmers and others who crossed the rivers frequently found that travel had become risky. Huge, untended flotillas of wood churned downstream, threatening to crush wagons or drown valuable stock at any moment. The smaller, denser ties, moreover, were difficult to tend in the water, and soon they were being rafted to Chicopee. Cook boats and work boats traveled with monster rafts of as many as fifteen hundred ties. The complete rafts were composed of blocks, each consisting of from thirty-five to fifty ties bound together by hickory poles fastened with forty-penny spikes. Those individual squares were then linked one to the next by another pole, allowing the articulation of the raft's sections as the barge snaked down the river. Bigger rafts ran to a thousand feet or more in length, putting the man on the front well out of sight and most likely around a bend in the stream from the snubber who rode the rear. The essential stern man jammed his snubbing pole through a slot built between the ties and then into the river bottom to slow the balky craft, while the man on the bow kept the raft off of shoals and away from the bank. The tendency of the dense oak to float low in the water kept the decks constantly awash and made maneuvering particularly difficult. Rafters, who sometimes built canvas sunscreens and casual chairs on the decks, took extra pay for their skill and bravado, earning as much as four dollars a day. Tight turns, like the one upstream from Van Buren at the place called Boat's Bend, splintered many rafts and left workers with crushed arms and legs. The power of the churning water, combined with the sheer mass of the lumber it carried, ruptured the Chinese Wall in 1902, sending some five thousand ties accumulated there in an irretrievable torrent downriver.

Each tie carried the logo of the company for which it had been cut and hacked; the symbol was applied to the oak with a hammer bearing the inverted design, much like a branding iron. Deadheads that sank to the bottom and were lost can occasionally be seen, resting in the clear water, the imprints still visible in their end grains.

By 1906, much of the timber easily accessible to Grandin, just east of the rivers and near the southern end of what is now Ozark National Scenic Riverways, had been sawed out. Scouts had found another forest on the lower Jacks Fork, and tramlines were laid into the woods there in 1907. At the end of the line, the company purchased the 200-acre farm of a man by the singular name of Shade Orchard. On that site they founded the town of West Eminence. Many of the buildings from the all but closed-out Grandin site were loaded onto flatcars and moved in their entirety to the new location. Work commenced on an all-new mill at West Eminence in 1909, and a year later the town was in place and the saws humming. The new community featured a bigger store, complete with soda fountain and ice cream parlor. A first-class baseball diamond, street lights, and fire hydrants marked the town as a trendy and up-to-the-minute place to live. Three hundred houses filled the townsite and residents enjoyed public debates, the music of traveling bands hired by the company, and community barbecues as diversions. The isolation, individuality, and self-sufficiency of the old Ozarker was slipping away.

The mill complex at West Eminence covered sixty acres, amid which two acres of drying shed was under roof, it being the practice of the day to dry for a minimum of ninety days even the poorest grades of lumber before shipping. The best grades, called B and Better, were kiln dried. Two saws, one circular blade and one band saw, turned out only one-third the capacity that had been available at Grandin. But mill operations were sophisticated and diversified, incorporating at one time the nation's only hub mill, which produced wagon-wheel hubs of the finest oak.

Mill workers at West Eminence accepted timber from the hills, cut it to boards, edged the lumber and sawed it to length, separated the various qualities, and shipped their products to market for ten years. In 1919, the Forked Leaf White Oak Company purchased the dwindling operation. All the big timber had been cut by that time, and little remained of the original forest. After the white and red oaks were taken, hickories and walnuts fell to the saws. New mills purchased the smaller pieces of wood for tool handles and barrel staves. The advent of trucks in the hills made reaching the more isolated stands economically

Idle since 1927, the old lumber mill at West Eminence stands in ruins. Only the boiler plant and fuel house remain to recall the immensity of the turn-of-the-century logging operation they supported.

feasible for individuals who competed with the big companies. In 1924, the millworks at West Eminence went into receivership.

The Current River Lumber Company bought the mill and made a last stab at running the centralized lumber plant profitably, operating until 1927 when the railroad tracks, boilers, and other hardware were finally sold for scrap. Portable sawmills that could be transported directly to cutting sites had by then appeared in the woods, making efficient competition all but impossible for the big firms with their huge overheads and outsized saws. Within a year, the Salem, Winona, and Southern Railroad announced the discontinuation of its fifteen-mile run from West Eminence to the major railhead at Winona for lack of lumber to haul and due to competition from good roads.

Lumbering activity continued, but at a greatly reduced pace, the region's people reluctant to accept the inevitable playing out of their windfall. Small operators sought isolated timber and cut it. Companies formed to exploit in new ways the wood that remained. The Egyptian Tie and Timber Company in 1931 opened a stave mill at Paint Rock Creek on the Current River where a small town was also built. The shorter pieces of oak required as barrel staves could not be rafted efficiently and only a few men with the necessary skills were able to manage johnboats laden with oak on the tricky river. For eight years the trio of Tom Moss, his son Ira, and Ray Randolph made names for themselves as legendary rivermen by loading their boats until only an inch of freeboard remained and hauling timber to mill.

Nevertheless, the last recorded log drive on the rivers came in 1935 and covered only the few pitiful miles from Cardareva to Beal's Landing as business dwindled to nothing. Because the rivers had been used so effectively for driving logs and rafting ties, they were considered legally navigable and therefore kept open for canoeing and johnboating; the Missouri Supreme Court established high-water marks as the boundary of public domain.

When the big lumber companies departed the region, a small percentage of those natives who had worked in the woods followed to the new cutting grounds in the Pacific Northwest. For most, the money simply dried up as quickly as it had come. There was little opportunity to succeed at a return to homesteading: rocky slopes remained in place of the lush forests; there was no forage and little wildlife; and a cash economy that turned on dollars had replaced the barter system. Many of the old ways were severely interrupted by the years of change and modernization. The fabric of tradition had been ripped. New elements of comfort, sophistication, and complexity had been introduced into the simpler order. More than an ancient forest disappeared on those railcars that visited the riverside during the fifty years from 1880 to 1930; more than a valuable resource was exploited.

Over the course of the following half-century a new forest was established across the devastated landscape. Great concern and effort were required to restore health to the land. Now, only widely scattered and unimpressive relics remain of the despoliation that claimed the old trunks. Tall, stout trees again grow in the woods where a misleading sense of inviolability has returned.

For the people facing their most difficult times, an innate resilience and a renewed closeness to the recovering land revived many of the traditional values that had always meshed so well with the distinctive nature of the countryside. Those who can remember firsthand the majesty of that original forest may be alone in comprehending all the changes that were suffered, but much of their heritage still graces the style and character of modern Ozark residents.

5.

Preservation

BY the time the rapacious timbering operations of the late nineteenth and early twentieth centuries moved west from the river hills, the countryside was forlorn and out of balance. Natural processes of regeneration and growth had long been throttled off, and the rivers had been altered by years of blasting to form channels for the transportation of logs. The large-scale cash economy first fostered by the lumber companies was left to die unsupported. If before it had required staunch commitment and toil to scratch a decent living from the rocky slopes, it then became almost impossible to provide just for one's self and one's family. In the span of fifty years, a land of virgin forest and premier habitat had been reduced to an expanse of cut-over snags and pebbles. The return of the balance that had operated on the land and the rivers is still pursued today.

When a tree is cut from the woods, many things change: more light strikes the forest floor where the leafy canopy is interrupted, fostering new and different growth; rain splashes harder onto the soil, impacting directly instead of slipping gently from the vegetation; rainwater runs off more quickly when the leaf litter that the tree once provided is no longer available; and roots that held soil in place die, loosening their grips and facilitating erosion. The cycle of harvest and regrowth is essential to a healthy forest, but when thousands of acres are clear-cut the effect is exponential, the result overwhelming.

Additionally, damage was caused to the woods by the many farmers who set fires each year to burn back the shoots and sprouts that competed with the desirable grasses for what few nutrients were available. The burning did do away with much of the competition and improved the browse in the woods. It may also have had some effect against those traditional Ozark pests—the tick and the chigger—as many farmers claimed, although the vast majority of those all-too-tough bugs undoubtedly survived even the heat of the spring fires.

The blazes did what they were set to do, but unfortunately their unanticipated side effects were more harmful than their primary purposes were beneficial. The burning off of the brush destroyed the leaf mold at work in the detritus on the forest floor and interrupted the processes of decay necessary to the improvement of soil fertility. Tree seedlings and other vegetation that would have replenished the green stock were charred and killed. Adopting the practice from the Indian culture, in which small fires were set to drive game or improve the grazing for the buffalo, the more numerous white men each year set thousands of acres ablaze.

Farmsteaders also held to their ways of turning stock out onto the open range. The hooves of their cattle, hogs, and horses compacted the soil and opened the way wider for the

On an icy winter's day, the water in the branch at Big Spring tumbles and steams on its thousand-foot trip to the river.

processes of erosion. Livestock competed head to head with wildlife for the dwindling forage. Interbreeding reduced the quality of the stock, and the proliferation of free-ranging animals was instrumental in killing out the bluestem grasses that had made the mountain landscape so parklike.

The changes in the environment wrought by man made it difficult for the domestic stock to thrive and almost impossible for more sensitive wildlife to survive. Hunting pressure combined with the degradation of the habitat to drive even the most common species from the hills.

As reminders of those days when open range was commonplace, U.S. Forest Service ranger stations in the area today keep in place their cattle guards and rail fences. The practice of setting stock free to roam the woods, long opposed by the Forest Service, ended only in the 1960s when state law denied all local option in the matter, although its popularity had been dwindling before then.

From 1910, the population of the mountains was in decline. Jobs were unavailable in a standstill economy, floods had become severe due to deforestation and accelerated runoff, and the battle for independence along the rivers appeared to many for the first time to have been decisively lost. Some made new attempts to wrest a living from the land, with the result that matters became generally worse rather than better. Moonshiners made bootleg whiskey at stills hidden in deep hollows. Previously unmarketable timber was sold for whatever price could be got. Gravel plants struggled to profit from the endless supply of chert that raced into the streams from the hills. And the practice of "grandma-ing"—in which poached timber was brought to market by those who owned no land yet claimed rights to a profit because the immature trees had come, they said, from grandma's property—appeared among some of the remaining timbermen.

The stripped ground, much of it still under lumber company ownership, went on the open market. Few Ozarkers fell for the offers, turning down the opportunity to purchase what they knew was devastated soil, proud of their savvy as judges of land quality. In cities to the north and east, the land was advertised as agricultural paradise—suitable for profitable orchards, lush strawberry fields, tomato plantations, and cattle and sheep ranches—or simply as private pieces of heaven in the wilds. Some of the schemes touted by the lumber companies' advertising men were actually tried by purchasers who soon discovered that Ozark clay could not be solidly relied upon to provide a profitable living.

Because of the tax liabilities involved, the companies were undoubtedly anxious to unload their holdings, sometimes offering prices as low as seven cents per acre. Without having provided for reforestation, they would have had to wait a full seventy-five-year rotation before again being able to harvest mature timber, paying taxes all the while. That, of course, they were not willing to do, and many taxes went unpaid.

While the lumber companies attempted to get out from under their holdings and the region's economy stagnated, other portions of the country had begun to recognize the need for protection from the ravages of unbridled exploitation. As early as the 1840s and 1850s a reverence for nature in its untamed state was espoused in the East by such original thinkers as Henry David Thoreau and John J. Audubon. To the West, the land which would eventually become Yosemite National Park was bequeathed to the state of California for protection

Ellington's Jefferson Hotel was constructed in a time of graceful architecture and relaxed tourism.

in 1864, and eight years later Yellowstone National Park was set up as the nation's first such preserve.

The populace responded with a conscience to the mistreatment of the land and sought to reestablish the balance that profiteering had upset. The pioneering movement was complete by 1890, and the nation's sympathies were turning away from the aggressive need to dominate and tame each new bit of wilderness encountered. The twentieth century opened amid the wave of the Progressive movement, accompanied by people with a new set of sensibilities, conservationists the likes of whom had never been seen before.

There came the outdoorsman President Teddy Roosevelt who established the first wildlife refuges, doubled the number of national parks, and quadrupled the size of the national forest; Gifford Pinchot, a Roosevelt appointee to the first American conservation commission and the nation's earliest professional forester; William Temple Hornaday, zoologist and promoter of laws for the protection of wildlife; and, a little later, Aldo Leopold, whose land ethic wove all of nature into a network of life.

To the Current River came Missouri Gov. Herbert S. Hadley, the first Republican elected to that office in many years and a man tagged with the nickname "The Mysterious Stranger." Hadley and a large contingent, smitten by the urge to visit the wilds, traveled to Welch Spring to take up there what was called an exploration party. On October 13, 1909, the group enjoyed a roast 'possum dinner before moving to a gravel bar where Ozark rivermen had constructed for them a number of johnboats to be employed on a float trip to Round Spring. Joining the governor on what was then almost a pure wilderness journey were influential businessmen, railroad executives, and reporters from Missouri's large newspapers. Despite the despoliation of the previous years, the scenic impact of the mountains was still strong and the resilient rivers ran clear. News of the trip broke across the state, calling attention to the Current River region. Controversy erupted following the historic trip, with one faction claiming that the land recently "discovered" should be preserved in its natural state, others suggesting that the area be developed as a recreation playground, and still more voices favoring further exploitation and the construction of dams to provide hydroelectric power.

This early conflict began a fifty-year tug-of-war over the future of the Current River country. Businessmen finally agreed that the rivers were too small and isolated to be of much value in the generation of power, so they were spared. It was widely noted, however, that not a single fish had been caught on the Hadley expedition, making the region suspect as any kind of lush wilderness.

As the state's interest focused on the natural beauty of the Ozarks, more people desired to see its wonders close-up. Tourists found their way to the streams, and the state undertook development of parks at Big Spring, Round Spring, Alley Spring, and Montauk Springs between 1920 and 1930. The same years produced a "good roads" amendment by the state legislature, allotting $60 million to the construction of better thoroughfares. Scarce funds left many of the parks underdeveloped, but the land had been set aside.

Canoes remained rare in the 1920s, with johnboats guided by local inhabitants still the rule on the waterways. In 1921, the Bales Boating and Mercantile Company was established at Eminence to assist anyone wishing to make a wilderness river trip. Three years later, Smalley's Motel opened to house visitors who came in an ever-increasing number of cars. Most roads were rough gravel, and drivers were forced to inch carefully across low-water

Clockwise, from top left: Herbalist, woodcarver, folk artist, and Shannon County fixture George Watson; Virgil Asberry, out of retirement to work as sawyer at a modern lumber mill; Alva and Bernice Bunch, longtime river-country residents; Ira Moss, riverman, with Festus, one of his best rabbit dogs.

Sorghum flourishes on the alluvial soil of the same stream bottoms that were once home to Osage Indian hunting camps.

The water-powered milling machines of the Alley Spring roller mill are operational today, almost a century after they were first installed. Uncommon craftsmanship and native yellow pine lumber distinguish the grain chutes.

crossings called hog-trough bridges for their resemblance to that barnlot feeder. An open view of running water on either side of the bridge and between the treads made the trip across exciting.

The Great Depression brought to the Ozarks an increase in population, as many of those who had wandered to jobs elsewhere returned to the hills to wait out tough economic times. The trend toward dwindling populations was only briefly reversed, however, reappearing after the thirties to hold sway until the exodus from the cities again brought large numbers during the 1960s and 1970s. The Depression ravaged an already flat economy, and again, as they had been so often in the past, the Ozark hollows were looked to as a retreat during times of difficulty.

All the while development was held in check by stagnant economic conditions, the natural environment gained time to recover. Left alone, the scars of exploitation began to heal, and native green returned to the forest. Where pine had been the dominant tree, quick-sprouting oaks took over and started to reclaim the woods. But the process was slow; the imbalance was so severe that the forces of regeneration struggled to gain a foothold. The scales had tipped far from center and healing alone could not undo the damage.

The Depression relief agencies that came to the Ozarks in force, combined with a growing conservation ethic, offered the extra help that was required. Wildlife received the support of the Missouri Department of Conservation, which worked to reestablish wild turkey and white-tailed deer populations by providing balanced habitat at a number of Ozark preserves. Much of the quality of the forest today is attributable to the work of state agencies, the Civilian Conservation Corps (CCC), and a young but progressive Forest Service.

Established under Roosevelt in 1905, the Forest Service began to acquire land around the rivers in 1934, when 10,442 acres were first purchased from the Moss Tie Company. Until 1933, state law effectively handcuffed the Forest Service by restricting the number of acres a federal agency could own in any one county. Those limits were lifted when the legislature saw the wisdom of reforestation programs preached by the Forest Service and Joel Bennett "Champ" Clark, senator from Missouri. Portions of the forest were named in honor of Senator Clark, not for William Clark of expeditionary fame as is so often assumed.

Reforestation made up most of the federal agencies' early work. With much labor supplied by workers from CCC camps, millions of shortleaf yellow pines were planted in the hills. The men of Camp F-8 near Winona planted more than two hundred thousand pines in 1940 alone. Young corpsmen were recruited from among the nations' many unemployed and received pay of thirty dollars per month for their labors in the wilds. Regulations required that at least twenty-two of that be sent home to dependents. The camps operated across the Ozarks until 1941, planting, building trails, and trapping wildlife for transportation to areas better suited to support the animals. The work was hard and the conditions rugged; year-round the men lived in tents and hauled their water by hand. Much of their labor involved the heavy tasks of construction with native stone. By their toil, the state parks of the region gained buildings, bridges, and spring branch channels.

Administering the planting was the Forest Service, which also worked to educate the people of the area concerning reforestation. Rangers encouraged private landowners to plant black walnut trees, which would grow to have great commercial value. They promoted the conversion of unproductive timberland to permanent pasture and spoke out against the practices of burning off the brush and turning stock animals loose. The popularity of the rangers was not universally high; many Ozark residents objected to the agency's presence in their hills and refused advice that went contrary to traditions. The uniformed men were considered to be outsiders and were treated with a suspicion born of previous encounters with newcomers promoting grand ideas. It took time for the Forest Service to demonstrate that its techniques of sound management could provide a sustained yield off the land through uses that helped to build the soil.

In 1939, Mark Twain National Forest was officially designated, setting aside a resource for the nation that now consists of more than 3 million acres of managed woodlands. Forest rangers remain a presence in the mountains where they still administer the land, continue to do some planting after evaluation procedures indicate the wisest use of the resource, and practice the Forest Service philosophy of multiple use.

In the mid-1930s, talk of damming the rivers began again when two reservoirs were proposed for the Current River by the U.S. Army Corps of Engineers as part of a flood-control plan for Missouri and Arkansas. Not far away, Lake Wappapello was under construction and scheduled for completion by 1941. In the southwestern corner of the state, Lake Taneycomo was complete by 1913 and prospering as a tourist attraction. Other Missouri dams to produce great recreation areas and generate hydroelectric power were also being promoted.

The suggestion that the Current River be dammed just downstream from Two Rivers and again near Doniphan, however, was opposed in the region and across the state as well. In Arkansas, where all of the benefits and none of the ill effects would have been felt, support for the flood-control plan was strong. But the proposal would have put both Big Spring and the town of Eminence under water. The rivers gave good accounts of themselves, running clear and inviting, and the country was too remote for Missourians to lend much support to the schemes of the developers. For a second time, the streams escaped a fate that was befalling others all around the country, a fate that would have left them irreversibly altered. Again, the mountains gained time to recover from the work of the sawyers.

Had the dams been built, the result might have been a fiasco in any case. The underground system of spring conduits and channels, combined with the many cave entrances to that network and the permeability of the ground, would have made effective damming almost impossible. The small amounts of power that might have been made at normal water levels would have had to travel great distances at substantial losses, and flood levels would have threatened the dams themselves.

Still, lakes under development nearby provided a constant reminder of the value of tourist dollars and kept the talk of damming alive. The protectors of the free-flowing streams fought to maintain the integrity of the river country they called home, and the conflict burned straight through the 1940s.

Then, in 1954, the Arkansas-Red-White River Basin Interagency Committee, established by President Truman to undertake a flood-control survey, released its historic study. The report made the revolutionary recommendation that the Current and the neighboring Eleven Point River be preserved in their natural states and that the two reservoirs under consideration be abandoned. Only two-and-a-half years later, the "Plan for Preservation and Development of Recreational Resources—Current and Eleven Point River Country, Missouri," was published and distributed. The product of collaboration by state and federal agencies, the plan was the conception of an idea that would be long in gestation, difficult in delivery.

Sound management techniques and a forest quick to regrow have combined to rejuvenate the forest products industry in the Ozarks. Sensible harvesting practices keep the woods healthy and productive.

Along the Ozark Trail, yellow pine seedlings planted during the 1930s have grown to replace the virgin forest that was cut from the hills.

Waste from a modern lumber mill, sawdust travels through pressurized pipes to its final resting place in a growing pile.

A mud bank on the lower Jacks Fork, scarred by erosion, stands in stark contrast to the rock-bound shores of the upper river.

Many in the affected region were taken aback by the sudden appearance of the document, unaware that consideration was being given their future by officialdom. Others looked with immediate favor upon the proposal to preserve the rivers and to develop recreation potentials. Battle lines were drawn in the hills. The depth of feelings expressed over the question of whether the Ozark rivers should be officially protected had much to do with the extent to which local opinion was considered in the decision-making processes that followed. Over the coming years, well-attended public hearings were often heated. Ozarkers saw to it that little escaped their scrutiny. If the past had sometimes left them exploited and isolated from national trends, this new issue thrust them to the forefront of public attention. And they were ready. Here, on Missouri turf, a new philosophy of preservation, a new concept to protect not just a parcel of particularly beautiful ground but an entire riverine system would be born. Involved in the process would be politicians and officials from all levels of government, conservationists of every stripe, and many Ozark residents both pro and con. No river had achieved such protected status before, and all the birth pains that could be expected to accompany a new form of governmental involvement in self-sufficient and independent lives were borne in the fray.

Official wheels turned slowly. In Washington and Jefferson City, representatives of the people struggled to define what was required in order to protect the rivers while leaving them as usable resources. In January 1959, the Missouri House of Representatives resolved to ask Congress to establish a national recreation area along the banks of the Current and the Eleven Point, declaring them to be national streams. Within one month the National Park Service, an agency whose involvement would later become critical, had drafted suggested legislation. But opposition voices insisted more study was required, and Missouri officials agreed. By June 1959, President Eisenhower had signed a bill allocating funds for a study of the region, and researchers opened an office in Jefferson City.

The result was the published recommendation that the Current, its tributary the Jacks Fork, and the Eleven Point rivers be included in a national monument of some 113,000 acres. The concept that the boundaries of the monument follow the courses of the streams and remain a mile or less in width while covering a length of 190 miles was unique. The report called the rivers "clean, strong and alive," and foresaw their administration as preserving "in public ownership an outstanding example of the Missouri Ozarks."

Governmental spokespersons promised that one of the basic purposes of any plan would be to preserve the wild beauty of the region. They offered this reassurance to those who feared the lopsided development of a playground, without provision for more traditional Ozark pursuits. Worried landowners formed the Current–Eleven Point Rivers Association, which, in July 1960 after much consideration, voted to oppose the creation of a national monument. They objected on the bases that there would almost certainly not be enough money made available to offer fair prices for land to be acquired, that ground would be removed from both productivity and taxation, and that the influx of tourists would threaten Ozark culture.

As the most organized critics of the plan to protect the rivers, the association wielded considerable political power. Behind them were many Ozark farmers and families to whom bottomland represented the only real wealth; that land was being threatened from the outside, and a fear of displacement took hold. Some worried that the government would take more land than was actually needed while either paying less than a fair price or simply exercising the power of condemnation. Others were concerned that only the good alluvial soils would be included in offers to buy, leaving farmers with just cherty slopes and no value to their farms. They had not forgotten that their predecessors had been run from their homes by bushwhackers during the Civil War and had suffered under the deals offered by the lumber companies. Some still harbored resentment from the early days of the national Forest Service, while other government-backed developments had displaced their friends and changed the face of the land forever with huge lake impoundments. It was no wonder that among the local inhabitants were those who stood firm in their opposition to any proposal that would alter the status quo.

The longtime pastor of an area church, who over the years aided many river-country families in times of need, wrote that he saw no moral justification for a project that would displace some people in order to fill the recreational desires of others. Joining the opposition at the outset was U.S. Rep. Richard Ichord, who provided a rallying cry for opponents when he reportedly uttered the statement, "I'm opposed to setting aside a large part of my district to make a habitat for bobcats and hoot owls."

But many, some along the rivers and some in the cities as well, foresaw growth encroaching on the unprotected streambanks and feared that honky-tonk developments, mass recreation for profit, and uncontrolled exploitation would soon spoil scenic values. They saw litter lining the banks and bottoms as usage levels increased and cabin colonies grew. Missouri naturalist Leonard Hall wrote of the possibility that the region would decline into a "permanent rural slum," in a 1960 newspaper column that called for a comprehensive conservation plan. Editors at the *St. Louis Post-Dispatch* agreed in a July 24, 1960, editorial, referring to the area as "just about the last outpost of true wilderness, not only in the Ozarks, but in the whole Midwest." Those who favored protection also cited a study promising that visitors to the park would add $5.5 million to the local economy annually and that $10 million would be added to assessed valuations of the counties in which new facilities were to be built.

A first attempt to pass legislation establishing an Ozark Rivers National Monument failed. Opponents pressured their representatives, and legislators found it difficult to reach agreement. At one time, three separate proposals were under consideration: one extreme calling for administration of federal land by a joint committee of local, state, and federal governments; the opposite pole holding out for full National Park status. Compromise, in all its sloth, promised the only solution. Conservationists cried that there remained little time to waste.

A boom in leisure, lightweight gear, and the spirit of the outdoors was rolling across the country, meanwhile. Americans headed for the woods, rivers, and mountains in record numbers. New developments in tents and sleeping bags and canoes made getting into the back country easier and more comfortable, and citizens in droves discovered the beauty of what remained of their homeland's wilderness. The rivers were sustaining ever larger numbers, many of whom knew little of the ethics of outdoor behavior.

Compromises were made to the proposal to protect the Current and the Eleven Point. Hunting would be allowed, retaining a right that had been so fundamental in the settling of the land. It was further agreed that involved property owners would be offered the chance to sell all of any plot consisting of 500 acres or less, thus assuring that farms would not be relieved of only their most productive ground. And the federal government would make payments to the counties in lieu of taxes lost.

As part of the unfolding drama, Secretary of the Interior Stewart Udall paid a visit to the Current River in September 1961 to assess the appropriateness of the area for inclusion in the park system. Along the Secretary's route were posted signs reading "Monument NO" in bold black letters against white backgrounds. Udall saw perhaps fifty of the signs nailed to trees on the course of his two-day trip. Visible to him from the air were five-foot-high limestone letters stretching a quarter-mile spelling out the same message. Opponents made their feelings known, but Udall fell in love nonetheless. Not put off by the display of local opinion, he recommended full national-park status for the rivers and vowed to put them "on every map." The Secretary's enthusiasm prompted further consideration and U.S. senators and other officials came to inspect the natural resource—the fate of which they would determine—as several more tours to the region were arranged. All were completed, somewhat surprisingly, without incident.

On January 14, 1963, U.S. Sen. Stuart Symington and Rep. Richard Ichord simultaneously introduced legislation to establish a park under the name Ozark National Rivers. The final compromise included land only along the Current and the Jacks Fork. Absent were any holdings in three of the counties originally considered, and the Eleven Point was also eliminated. The Senate quickly adopted the bill. After setting a limit on acreage and changing the name to Ozark National Scenic Riverways, the House too approved the bill. On August 27, 1964, President Lyndon B. Johnson signed into law the act preserving for the first time an American river system.

By mid-1966 the first tract of land had been purchased from private ownership, and a year later the land acquisition office at Eminence had bought seventy-six hundred acres. The state signed over ownership of the state parks at Alley, Round, and Big springs in 1969. Retained by the state were the park and trout hatchery at Montauk. The state also maintained ownership of many of the lands near the rivers in state forest and natural areas. Dedication of the river park came in 1972 when Tricia Nixon Cox appeared for ceremonies at Big Spring. By that time, 88 percent of the projected land had been acquired and $7 million had been spent. George Hartzog, then Director of the National Park Service and a stalwart promoter of the river park for years, said at the dedication that the streams were "the great treasure of the National Park Service."

The successful struggle to protect the two rivers opened the way for additional legislation. Just a year after signing the Ozark bill, President Johnson said, "The time has come to identify and preserve free-flowing stretches of our greatest scenic rivers before growth and development make the beauty of the unspoiled waterway a memory. To this end I will shortly send to Congress a bill to establish a national wild rivers system." That promise evolved into the National Wild and Scenic Rivers Act of 1968, godchild of the Ozark legislation and protector of eight rivers initially, including the Eleven Point. More streams have since been added to the system, and many remain candidates for inclusion.

As it assumed management of the Riverways, the National Park Service was confronted with wildly increasing numbers of users, their attendant impact on the resource, and, be-

Named for a Choctaw Chief who led his tribe through the area, Cardareva Bluff flanks the Current River. The Indian leader is said to be buried near the summit of the mountain that also bears his name.

From a bluff overlooking the river, well-defined pastures mark a farmer's staked-out claim. (Overleaf)

cause it was the first of its kind, no accepted baseline from which to develop plans for management. The voices that had warned of tourists thronging to the Ozark wilds upon official designation of park status had been correct. But perhaps they were not quite so accurate as those who had said that the hordes were coming whether or not a management agency was in place and that the land's ultimate destiny would be much improved were a capable overseer empowered to exercise control. Whether the people came because a strip was suddenly colored light green on their maps or because of an accelerating interest in all outdoor pursuits is an unanswered question. From whatever motivation, visits continue to increase. The Riverways in 1984 is within a comfortable day's drive for 20 million people, and there can no longer be any doubt that, in summer anyway, the solitude that once enhanced a river experience here is gone.

Before developing patterns of use could be managed, they had to be identified. With river access available at fifty places, simple methods of counting users were not possible, so special techniques had to be developed. Employing timing devices and telephoto lenses to allow camera placement away from the rivers, researchers were able to count canoeists without intruding on their anonymity or recreation.

The collected figures reveal that in 1979 slightly fewer than 2 million people visited the Riverways and that the number had increased steadily from 1972 at an average rate of 5 percent per year. In 1982, the number of visits held steady at 1.9 million. Of all those who used the rivers, 90 percent came during the months of April through September, and 55 percent of the visits occurred in the three months of June, July, and August. Such figures suggest how likely Americans are to love their wildernesses to death by concentrating their numbers and their visits on relatively small areas within brief spans of time.

Figures for use by canoeists showed similar if more dramatic increases and imbalances. During the early years of the park, canoeist days jumped by slightly more than 10 percent per year until in 1979 the Current and Jacks Fork together supported 290,000 canoeist days. Figures for 1982 reflect an increase in canoeing of 6 percent from the previous year, to 308,000 canoeist days on the water. By dividing the rivers into zones, researchers were able to discover that on the Current the three accesses of Akers, Pulltite, and Round Spring handle 65 percent of the total use; the lower river remains more lightly used. On the Jacks Fork, almost 90 percent of the floater traffic is confined to the miles between Alley Spring and Two Rivers, much of which lies outside park boundaries because space was allowed for the expansion of towns such as Eminence and Van Buren when the Riverways' limits were drawn.

Analyzing their data, experts found that nearly 50 percent of all canoeists arrived from St. Louis and that usage of the streams by area residents accounted for only 1.1 percent of the total. That represents a significant change from twenty years earlier when almost every boat contained at least one Ozark riverman as a guide. Almost 70 percent of all river trips now last only a day, and approximately 90 percent of the boaters rent their craft in the area. Revealingly, nearly two-thirds of the canoeists travel in large groups of at least ten people. Such grouping has been shown to have an inordinate effect on the environment.

The data compiled provide a base from which the Park Service hopes to meet the needs of the most users. And while results might be initially discouraging to the purist who seeks a wilderness experience, they can actually help to identify those seasons of the year and parts of the rivers that still offer solitude. Disheartening as the thought of a thousand aluminum canoes on fifteen miles of water might be, the knowledge that numbers are five times as great on Saturday as on any weekday suggests an avenue to relief.

Winter's chill captures water seeping from a bedding plane in the rock and freezes it into a curtain of icy towers.

Changes in the direction of the river's flow are the rule rather than the exception, and it is common for the canoeist to find an unyielding rock at the apex of every turn.

A five-second photographic exposure depicts Alley Spring's flow as a collection of parallel, jewelled strands.

The information collected by park staff and contractors has been condensed and codified to produce a general management plan, which recognizes that the rivers and the 80,080 acres composing the park have distinct carrying capacities that limit use. As resilient as the country is and despite the fact that seven months of minimal use each year provide a period for regeneration, degradation does result where too many feet tread. To that end, the document calls for continued and expanded testing of water quality to monitor sedimentation and pollution levels. The rivers themselves will tell immediately should problems arise. And because use is highly concentrated, it is easy for rangers to check areas of overuse and to close them temporarily for repair or renewal.

Park naturalists agree that the land is so tough and that the rivers do so much to cleanse their banks each year that determining the physical carrying capacity and drawing a line beyond which use must be regulated is more difficult than if the environment were a fragile tundra or a more delicately balanced rain forest. There, protection would be required at every turn; here, only rarely.

So, too, the biological carrying capacity is difficult to determine. The vast majority of users gets no farther from the streambed or campground than a few yards, allowing an undisturbed buffer in near-wilderness for most wild species. Studies of fish and their responses to increasing boat traffic have failed to show that canoeing pressure influences spawning or other behavior. Much more study of these and other issues is called for in the management plan.

With regard to the psychological carrying capacity, an existing problem is acknowledged. Surveys made along the most heavily used portions of the two rivers reveal that 61 percent of those contacted experienced more crowding than they desired. That figure, from 1979, doubled the number who had offered the same opinion seven years earlier.

With that increasing dissatisfaction in mind, park officials determined to gain control of patterns of use that had developed largely uninfluenced. As early as 1975 the Park Service attempted to limit commercial renting of canoes in the region, but the efforts were thwarted in the courts; the regulations were adjudged too vague. A recent ruling reversed that setback when the courts agreed that the Park Service should have the power to issue permits controlling commercial operations affecting the park. In practice, the ruling empowers the Park Service to limit the rental of canoes by requiring any rental outfit to be in possession of a permit. There are currently seventeen permittees and two larger contractors recognized to provide canoes for use in the park; together they offer for rent 1,719 boats. The Park Service hopes the issue of control, fought long and hard by those with canoes to rent and a desire to do business, is now largely settled. They hope to manage use of the water more effectively by maintaining a limit on the number of canoes to be rented. The management plan, however, holds out the possibility that individual permits for each boat on the river might be required if all else fails to bring crowding under control. Such a system is employed in the Grand Canyon, where the nation's most restrictive camping remains popular.

The plan also anticipates the expenditure of more than $11 million at twenty-one sites within the boundaries of the Riverways. That development is expected to aid in the redistribution of usage as well. The expenditures will follow a more modest but still substantial development program undertaken in 1974 when campgrounds were improved and the Powder Mill Visitor's Center was constructed. Unfortunately, the building at Powder Mill lies outside the zones of heavy use and has therefore attracted only a fraction of the Riverways' visitors.

In the Rexall drugstore in Eminence, the floor is wood, the scale takes a penny, and the stools still spin.

Though it is somewhat presumptuous to speak for them, a portion of the local population has yet to give up its fight against what is still seen as meddling by the federal government. There are those who continue to oppose the park and its operation and who willingly cite difficulties encountered by and with the Park Service. Occasional references to the many one-day canoeists drawn to the rivers as "undesirables" can be heard. Some claim the fishing has been ruined and that they are now unable to use johnboats when confronted by flotillas of tubers who choke the waterways in rented innertubes, the largest crowds invariably near the best put-in spots for powerboats. Complaints continue to include the belief that families who lived for generations along the banks, raised children there, and were proud of their fine farms have now been put off the land, that the money received for bottomland could never have been enough. Moreover, new regulations that limit outboard motors to forty horsepower and restrict the use of firearms solely to in-season hunting keep the pot of discontent boiling in southern Missouri.

It is not uncommon for the National Park Service, new to an area, to encounter resistance; other people in other places have waged local battles. But few have done so with the tenacity and continued aggressiveness of those Ozarkers who refuse to accept this newest bureaucracy in their lives. It is unlikely that those who continue to differ with the Park Service will, in this generation, mend their disagreements.

Still, all but the most stubborn admit that litter on the rivers has been reduced below the bothersome level it had reached before the influx of tourists and that the number of crossings over the two streams remains unchanged without new development or bankside clutter to mar the scene from a boat seat. As the Park Service pursues its policy of letting unused roads go unrepaired and as much of the watershed returns to natural vegetation, a more wilder-nesslike feeling creeps into every boat trip. And there can be no argument that the Riverways' fifty-four permanent and ninety-six seasonal employees pump almost $2 million directly into the local economy each year. Another million dollars come from contracts for goods and services let locally. Tourist spending contributes to the health of the economy, even if the anticipated boom never quite materialized.

Despite the occasional misstep, the administration of the park struggles toward an elusive balance between visitor use for which they must provide and the preservation of the streams in a natural state. The Park Service's most frequently referred to guide in that effort is the enabling legislation that established the Riverways. It makes clear the charge that the environment must, as a first priority, be protected.

The streams are called upon to provide recreation of every conceivable sort. There exists a broad chasm between those who enjoy a river trip as a floating beer party at which the sounds of nature amount to the clang of another empty landing in an aluminum canoe and their opposite numbers who desire a quiet venue for spiritual renewal amid the again-abundant wildlife. But the rivers satisfy both, as well as everyone between. By choosing time and place, any visitor to the Ozark National Scenic Riverways can find whatever outdoor experience he seeks from among what the land and water make available.

The Current and the Jacks Fork may, in the last analysis, be as good a place as any for the many to find their individually defined outdoor experiences. The land is diverse, home to a multitude of species and assorted wonders. Few people can escape a confrontation with the value of wild country during a trip amid such a profusion of natural workings. And it is a tough place, capable of rebuffing all but the most devastating attacks of man. It renews itself well, overcoming much of the degradation inflicted upon it. And little alteration of its

Old railroad pilings still poke from the water, recalling turn-of-the-century logging operations.

Carefully selected native stones form the walls of the old Cedargrove school building.

Darkness settles on the tree-lined rivers even before the sunset fades.

wild state needs to be considered to make even the most inexperienced outdoorsman safe in the hills or on the water.

That the rivers sustain so many expectations and invite so many uses may, instead of working to their eventual detriment, turn out to be their saving grace. Here, many people with a wide range of concerns watch over the same land. The National Park Service, the U.S. Forest Service, and the state of Missouri cooperate to protect the region professionally. Local hunters, fishermen, and landowners stay ever alert to their own special claims. Conservationist organizations remain proud and possessive of the parklands. And families and church groups think of the rivers as their own, returning each year to float a favorite stretch of water. Like the theory of genetic diversity that says the variety of species it will support is indicative of an ecosystem's healthfulness, the kaleidoscope of interests reflected in the waters of the Current and the Jacks Fork suggests a long and healthy future.

It is unsafe to assume, however, that because the rivers have achieved federal protection they are safe forever. There exist examples aplenty in which such protection has proved powerless to effect true preservation. On at least one of the nation's wild rivers, mining effluents entering a tributary creek from beyond the boundaries of protection fouled the water. Given the nature of the watershed, a similar horror could easily befall the Current or the Jacks Fork. Changing patterns of use, new and unsympathetic expectations, and encroaching development at the borders all conceivably threaten the future sanctity of the Riverways. Complacency opens the way for such a horrific vision.

But there is no complacency where these streams are concerned, as they are tugged this way and that by such varied users, every one as possessive as the next. As long as each interest keeps peeled its watchful eye, these two Ozark rivers stand to benefit and perhaps eventually to regain that balance of which they have been deprived.

Bibliographical Note

THE sources consulted in the preparation of this text are of a wide variety, ranging from personal interviews through government studies to published volumes of scholarly stature. Some of the most engaging sources are those pertaining to past inhabitants of the Current River country. One particularly observant early visitor, Henry Rowe Schoolcraft, was among the few to set down the details of life amid the Osage Indians and the first trappers and hunters. In 1821 he published *Journal of a Tour into the Interior of Missouri and Arkansas from Potosi or Mine in Burton, in Missouri Territory, in a Southwestern Direction, Toward the Rocky Mountains, Performed in the Years 1818–1819* (London: Sir Richard Phillips and Co., 1821). As his title suggests, Schoolcraft was a deliberate and often opinionated author who nonetheless makes interesting reading. A more contemporary writer, John J. Mathews, has added greatly to what is known of the Osage Indians and their ways with his unusually complete *The Osages: Children of the Middle Waters* (Norman: University of Oklahoma Press, 1961). Mathews is also the author of *Wah' Ken-Tah: The Osage and the White Man's Road* (Norman: University of Oklahoma Press, 1968). An equally useful representation of Ozark cultures is *The Ozarks: Land and Life* (Norman: University of Oklahoma Press, 1980) by Milton D. Rafferty. With specific emphasis on archaeology and early cultures, two brief but excellent works are *Indians of Upper Current River* (Eminence, Mo.: 1978) by Alan Banks, and Carl H. Chapman and Eleanor F. Chapman's *Indians and Archaeology of Missouri,* rev. ed. (Columbia: University of Missouri Press, 1983). A more general sourcebook, *The History of Missouri* (New York: Lewis Historical Publishing Co., 1967) by David D. March offers a glimpse into the lives of past Missourians.

Concerning the topics of geology and geologic events, J. Harlen Bretz's justifiably famous *Caves of Missouri* (Rolla: Missouri Geological Survey and Water Resources, 1956) continues to set the standard as it has since its publication. Also useful is Bretz's *Geomorphic History of the Ozarks of the State of Missouri* (Rolla: Missouri Geologic Survey and Water Resources, 1965). Still another classic in its field, Carl Ortwin Sauer's *The Geography of the Ozark Highland of Missouri* (New York: AMS Press, 1920), chronicles the physical features and the processes that created them. Enlightening comment on the area's geology can also be found in *The Geology of Missouri* (Columbia: University of Missouri Press, 1944) by E. B. Branson. A wealth of otherwise unattainable information relating to the state's many springs is easily located in the thorough research of Jerry D. Vineyard and Gerald L. Feder, *Springs of Missouri* (Rolla: Missouri Geological Survey and Water Resources, 1974).

More than just handbooks, Edgar Dennison's *Missouri Wildflowers* (Jefferson City: Missouri Department of Conservation, 1978) and Carl Settergren and R. E. McDermott's *Trees of Missouri* (Columbia: University of Missouri Agricultural Experiment Station, 1977) discuss the many plant species that can be found throughout the Ozark forest. The interrelationship and successions of those plants are the subjects of Julian A. Steyermark's *Vegetational History of the Ozark Forest* (Columbia: University of Missouri Press, 1959).

Of importance for their emphasis on the fauna of the Ozark mountains are a number of publications. A storehouse of information is contained in William L. Pflieger's *The Fishes of Missouri* (Jefferson City: Missouri Department of Conservation, 1975), which provides general data as well as specifics concerning every species of fish common to Missouri waters. *The Birds of America* (New York: Macmillan, 1965) by John James Audubon, *Birds in Our Lives* (Washington, D.C.: Bureau of Sport Fisheries and Wildlife, U.S. Department of the Interior, 1966) edited by Alfred Stefferud, and *A Field Guide to the Birds East of the Rockies*, 4th ed. (Boston: Houghton Mifflin, 1980) by Roger Tory Peterson offer the layperson many insights into the habits of the winged residents of these watersheds. More specific is A. W. Schorger in *The Wild Turkey: Its History and Domestication* (Norman: University of Oklahoma Press, 1966).

For a more scientific consideration of some of the streams' properties, the student should consult Hugh C. Clifford, *Some Limnological Characteristics of Six Ozark Streams* (Jefferson City: Missouri Department of Conservation, 1966); E. H. Sandhaus and John Skelton, *Magnitude and Frequency of Missouri Floods* (Rolla: Missouri Geologic Survey and Water Resources, 1969); and John L. Funk, *Missouri's Fishing Streams* (Jefferson City: Missouri Department of Conservation, 1968). A wider ranging but equally fascinating compendium of many facts concerning the character of the Ozarks and the state at large is Milton D. Rafferty's *Historical Atlas of Missouri* (Norman: University of Oklahoma Press, 1981); for quick reference to an assortment of information, no volume offers more.

From the perspective of wilderness and the need within each of us to experience wild surroundings, Roderick Nash's reasoning in *Wilderness and the American Mind,* 3d ed. (New Haven and London: Yale University Press, 1982) is original and precedent setting. No author has done more to clarify the involved relationship between Americans and their wild lands. Nash guided the author's thinking on the ways in which the Current and the Jacks Fork fit into an evolving national conservation ethic. In a similar context, *The National Parks* (New York: Alfred A. Knopf, 1968) by Freeman Tilden adds perspective to any regional view.

In a class by themselves are those works consulted less for factual or historical research than for spiritual and thematic guidance. The Ozarks are unique, and it is easy to become engrossed in those details that set them apart, thus losing sight of the larger picture. For help in maintaining a proper perspective, the author found especially valuable the works of the well-respected Missouri naturalist Leonard Hall: particularly enlightening is *Earth's Song* (Columbia: University of Missouri Press, 1981) and always enjoyable is *Stars Upstream: Life Along an Ozark River,* rev. ed. (Columbia: University of Missouri Press, 1969). Additional guides include *The Boomtown of West Eminence and Its Lumbering Days* edited by Judy Ferguson (Rolla: Rolla Printing Co., 1969) and Margaret Ray Vickery's reminiscence of times gone by, *Ozark Stories of the Upper Current River* (Salem, Mo.: Salem News, n.d.) Also inspiring are the many works of Vance Randolph, longtime chronicler of the lighter side of Ozark life. Randolph's *We Always Lie to Strangers* (Westport, Conn.: Greenwood Press, 1951) is a particularly readable example of his many works.

Government Publications

During the years since the U.S. Government first became interested in the Current and Jacks Fork rivers, federal employees and contractors have studied many aspects of the streams. Their original research has been exceptionally important to this text.

One of the earliest documents prepared under governmental auspices, *Ozark Rivers National Monument—A Proposal* (Washington, D.C.: United States Department of the Interior, National Park Service, 1960) presents a first vision of a park along the rivers.

Two reports prepared for the National Park Service focus on the resource of the area's caves, scrutinizing them in great detail. *Cave Resources at Ozark National Scenic Riverways: An Inventory and Evaluation* (Jefferson City: Missouri Department of Conservation, 1983) by James E. Gardner and John T. Taft and *Cave Management Investigations on the Ozark National Scenic Riverways, Missouri* (Protem, Mo.: Ozark Underground Laboratories, 1980) by speleologist Thomas J. Aley both provide details on specific caves and explanations of the geologic processes associated with cave building.

In the same fashion, William J. Wagner's *Alley Spring Roller Mill* (National Park Service, Historic Structure Report, n.p., n.d.) presents that building's past in the context of a broader history. Also concerned with the human history of the region and of immense importance to the research are David L. Fritz's *Historic Resources Study as Part of the Cultural Resources Management Section of the General Management Plan for the Ozark National Scenic Riverways* (Denver: National Park Service, 1979) and Lenard E. Brown's *History—Basic Data—Ozark National Scenic Riverways* (National Park Service, Division of History, 1969). For still another insightful presentation of the region's history, the interested reader should not overlook the *Overview of Cultural Resources in the Mark Twain National Forest, Missouri,* 4 vols. (Springfield: Center for Archaelogical Research, Southwest Missouri State University, 1979). Sections of the overview were authored by Mary Lee Douthit, Robert E. Cooley, Barbara Fisher, Lynn Morrow, and perhaps the foremost of all Ozark scholars, Robert Flanders.

More ancient matters are the concern of *Archeological Resources at Ozark National Scenic Riverways* (Lincoln, Nebr.: National Park Service, Midwest Archeological Center, 1981) by archaeologist Mark J. Lynott. Lynott supervises archaeological investigations on the rivers each summer and has unearthed startling discoveries.

A dismaying picture of the use the two rivers receive today is painted by researchers Leo Marnell, David Foster, and Kenneth Chilman in a report entitled *River Recreation Research at Ozark National Scenic Riverways; 1970–1977* (Van Buren, Mo.: National Park Service, 1978). Full of diagrams and figures, the study is an in-depth assessment of users and displays a highly imaginative research design. Partly as a result of what the recreation study showed, the *Environmental Assessment* (Denver: National Park Service, 1980) and the *Draft General Management Plan* (Denver: National Park Service, 1981) go to some length to propose safeguards for the rivers and their watersheds. The two documents were prepared by the staff of Ozark National Scenic Riverways, professionals at the National Park Service's Denver Service Center, and other employees of the Department of the Interior.

For all its emphasis on the history of the region, no single effort by the Park Service has been more important than the preservation of interviews with those who can recall the days before modernization swept the hills. Little of the old Ozark culture was permanently recorded, and only hill folks born and raised in the mountains possess much of the vital historical information. The Riverways' Oral History Program preserves in transcript form much of what otherwise would have been lost. *Two Ozark Rivers* owes a great deal to the voluminous oral history files and to the natives who granted permission for their tales to be included here. Drawn from were the interviews with Leo Anderson, Bertha Boyher, Henry Boyher, Walter Carr, Carl Frazier, Leonard Hall, Lillie Howell, Mariam McSpadden, Louise Smalley Randolph, Ray Randolph, Edna Staples, and Molly Summers.

Also invaluable in researching the events leading up to the establishment of the National Park was the file at park headquarters in Van Buren devoted to the administrative history of Ozark National Scenic Riverways. Newspaper and magazine clippings there form a diverse group of sources. Major contributors to the file include Eminence's *Current Wave* newspaper, the *St. Louis Post-Dispatch,* the *St. Louis Globe-Democrat,* the *Kansas City Times,* the *Memphis Press-Scimitar,* and other nearby newspapers.

Other Periodicals

The state of Missouri is blessed with one of the nation's finest conservation agencies. Among the many efforts of the Missouri Department of Conservation is its monthly magazine, *Missouri Conservationist.* In almost every issue can be found at least one article of interest to anyone concerned with the rivers and the web of life they support. Equally informative in its own province is *The Missouri Archaeologist.*

Interviews

Interviews with those people who know the rivers either professionally or in their Ozark bones filled the gaps left among other research and added life to the text. All of the conversations relating to this book were held during 1983, at the interviewees' private homes and offices, in caves, and at bankside.

Ira and Myrtle Moss have lived their entire lives on the rivers, and Ira has often depended upon them for a living. Together they know the streams as well as anyone. They were graciously hospitable and answered many questions, often clarifying confusion left by conflicting published accounts. The Mosses' good friend Louise Smalley Randolph was another source of information often overlooked in published histories. Mr. and Mrs. Ira Helvey recalled the logging days and the construction of a ferry boat at Powder Mill during an interview held on their front porch, which looks out over the remains of the old lumber mill

Pulltite Spring's cool flow meanders toward the river.

in West Eminence. And naturalist Leonard Hall, a principal in the fight to gain protection for the rivers, contributed his wisdom freely.

Owner of a canoe livery and store at Round Spring, businessman Gary Smith has witnessed big changes on the rivers with the coming of notoriety and a national park. Ernie Middleton, a boat and innertube renter, described for the author some of his beliefs and opinions.

At Montauk State Park, Park Superintendent Pete Landstad, Assistant Superintendent Charles Hesse, and Hatchery Manager Tom Perry were kind enough to explain their operation and a portion of the regional history. The finer points of karst topography were carefully made clear in interviews with Art Hebrank, a geologist with the Missouri Department of Natural Resources, Division of Geology and Land Survey. And Mike Pyles, sub-district ranger at Round Spring, Ozark National Scenic Riverways, added his valuable information in a second tour of Round Spring Caverns.

During a visit to a streamside archaeological excavation, Mark J. Lynott, supervisory archaeologist for the National Park Service, detailed for the author much of the progression that occurred among ancient cultures near the rivers. Also interviewed at the dig were Missouri archaeologists James and Cynthia Price.

Staff members at Ozark National Scenic Riverways spend their workdays dealing with the natural resources of the park and the many people who take advantage of its wealth. They develop specialized knowledge available nowhere else. Park Superintendent Arthur Sullivan helped provide an understanding of park operations and future plans, while Management Assistant Dean Einwalter was kind enough to fill in details and numbers. Most helpful with both park policy and the history of the area was historian Jere Krakow, with whom the author spent many hours engaged in conversation. Not enough can be said for the assistance of Dr. Krakow and his co-workers Alex Outlaw, chief of the Division of Interpretation, and Christopher M. White, supervisory park ranger–naturalist. Together, they provided much information and enormous assistance.

And several interviews with Frank Koenig added yet another perspective to the author's approach. Koenig is district ranger for the U.S. Forest Service, Winona District, Fristoe Unit, Mark Twain National Forest, with offices at Winona, Missouri.